# MIT ENGLISCHAUFGABEN DURCHS SCHULJAHR

## Wortschatz zu Farben, Zahlen & Co. sicher trainiert – Klasse 3/4

Für den Einsatz im Wochenplan
inkl. Lösungen

Ricarda Dransmann
Svenja Sölter

Verlag an der Ruhr

# Impressum

**Titel**
Mit Englischaufgaben durchs Schuljahr –
Wortschatz zu Farben, Zahlen & Co. sicher trainiert – Klasse 3/4
*Für den Einsatz im Wochenplan, inkl. Lösungen*

**Autorinnen**
Ricarda Dransmann
Svenja Sölter

**Umschlagmotiv**
Foto: © bongkarn – stock.adobe.com

**Illustrationen**
Anja Boretzki, soweit nicht anders angegeben

**Druck**
AZ Druck und Datentechnik GmbH, Kempten, DE

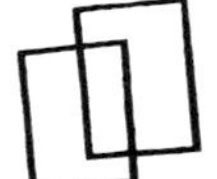

**Verlag an der Ruhr**
Mülheim an der Ruhr
www.verlagruhr.de

**Geeignet für die Klassen 3–4**


**ISBN 978-3-8346-4768-9**

# Inhaltsverzeichnis

# Vorwort

Mit „fix und fertigen“ Englisch-Hausaufgaben durchs Schuljahr – genau so einfach, wie es sich liest, möchten wir es Ihnen mit diesen Materialien machen. Ohne viel Erklärungs- und Kopieraufwand können Sie den Schüler*innen Hausaufgaben mit auf den Weg geben, und zwar nicht nach jeder Stunde, sondern für ein ganzes Themenfeld über einen längeren Zeitraum – in der Gesamtheit sogar für nahezu alle Themenfelder, die der Kernlehrplan für den Englischunterricht in der Grundschule vorgibt.

Vor allem für die Lehrkräfte, die mit einem Wochenplan oder Arbeitsplan arbeiten, passt diese Umsetzungsform hervorragend zur allgemeinen Unterrichtsplanung.

Wir bieten Ihnen Kopiervorlagen zu 17 Themenkomplexen, wobei jeder Themenkomplex zwei Seiten umfasst. Zwei Themenkomplexe erwiesen sich als sehr gut kombinierbar („numbers & colours“, „fruit & vegetables“), wodurch der zusätzliche Zweig „mixed“ entstand. Zusätzlich findet sich je eine Seite mit Übungen zu „Christmas“ und „Easter“.

Bei der Erstellung haben wir im Speziellen darauf geachtet, möglichst selbsterklärende Aufgaben zu verwenden, um den Kindern auch in dem Fach Englisch die Möglichkeit zu geben, ohne große Erklärung durch die Lehrkraft in den Arbeitsprozess einzutauchen. Zudem eignen sich die Aufgaben so auch wunderbar für Wochenplanarbeit oder aber das Homeschooling.

**So geht's:**
Reichen Sie Ihren Schüler*innen eine der vorgesehenen Kopiervorlagen zu einem Thema und lassen Sie sie über einen festen Zeitraum die Aufgaben bearbeiten.

Die Bearbeitung muss sich hierbei trotz des Begriffs „Wochenplan“ nicht auf eine Woche erstrecken, sondern kann auch einen längeren Zeitraum umfassen. Die „normale“ Woche wird schließlich häufig durch Feiertage, Schulaktivitäten oder Ähnliches unterbrochen und zudem werden durch geringe Wochenstundenzahlen die Themenkomplexe im Englischunterricht nicht in einer Woche abgehandelt. Den Bearbeitungszeitraum können Sie also ganz flexibel festlegen. Die Kinder tragen diesen Zeitraum oben unter „work schedule from … to …“ ein. Das gibt Ihnen als Lehrkraft sowie auch den Kindern, Eltern und ggf. den Mitarbeitenden im Offenen Ganztag eine gewisse Verlässlichkeit. Die Kinder haben zudem die Möglichkeit, sich die Bearbeitung der Aufgaben im vorgegebenen Zeitraum frei einzuteilen.

Pro Kopiervorlage stehen den Kindern vier Aufgaben zu einem Themenfeld zur Verfügung. Insgesamt umfasst ein Themenfeld (mit Ausnahme der „mixed“-Übungen sowie „Christmas“ und „Easter“) acht Aufgaben auf zwei Arbeitsblättern. Die Kinder dokumentieren ihre Bearbeitung, indem sie das Datum notieren und die erledigten Aufgaben abhaken.

Zur (Selbst-)Kontrolle können Sie die vorgegebenen Lösungen (ab S. 45) einsetzen und die Person, die die Aufgabe kontrolliert, kann dort einen entsprechenden Haken setzen. Je nach Leistungsstand können viele Kinder ihre Aufgaben mithilfe der Lösungen gut selbst kontrollieren.

Wir wünschen viel Freude bei der Arbeit mit unseren Englisch-Hausaufgaben!
*Ricarda Dransmann & Svenja Sölter*

---

*Der Verlag an der Ruhr legt großen Wert auf eine geschlechtergerechte und inklusive Sprache. Daher nutzen wir das Gendersternchen, um sowohl männliche und weibliche als auch nichtbinäre Geschlechtsidentitäten einzuschließen. Alternativ verwenden wir neutrale Formulierungen.*

# AUFGABEN FÜR DEN ARBEITSPLAN

**vegetables** page 2

name: ...................................

work schedule from .................... to ....................

1. Tick ✓ the right box.

☐ mushroom

☐ onion
☐ pepper
☐ radish

☐ cauliflower
☐ potato
☐ radish

| C | S | L |
|---|---|---|
| A | A | E |
| R | O | T |
| R | B | T |
| O | N | U |
| T | W | C |
| O | M | E |

done on: .......... checked ☐

**colours** page 1

name: ...................................

work schedule from .................... to ....................

1. Read and colour.

blue green red yellow orange pink

black grey white purple brown colourful

done on: .......... checked ☐

2. Find the colour words. Circle.

bluegreenyellowpinkblackredpurpleorangewhitebrown

done on: .......... checked ☐

3. Read and colour.

a green apple — a black car — a brown cat

a purple present — a grey mouse — a red and blue ball

done on: .......... checked ☐

4. Write down the English words.

grün .................... rot .................... weiß ....................

gelb .................... blau .................... braun ....................

schwarz .................... orange .................... lila ....................

done on: .......... checked ☐

8 MIT ENGLISCHAUFGABEN DURCHS SCHULJAHR

name: ..........

work schedule from .......... to ..........

**1. Draw lines.**

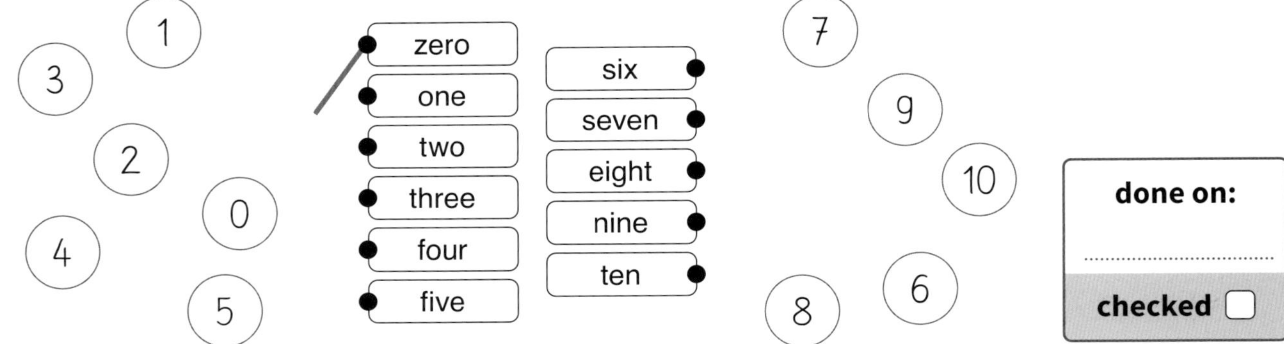


**done on:** ..........

**checked** ☐

**2. Write down the number words.**

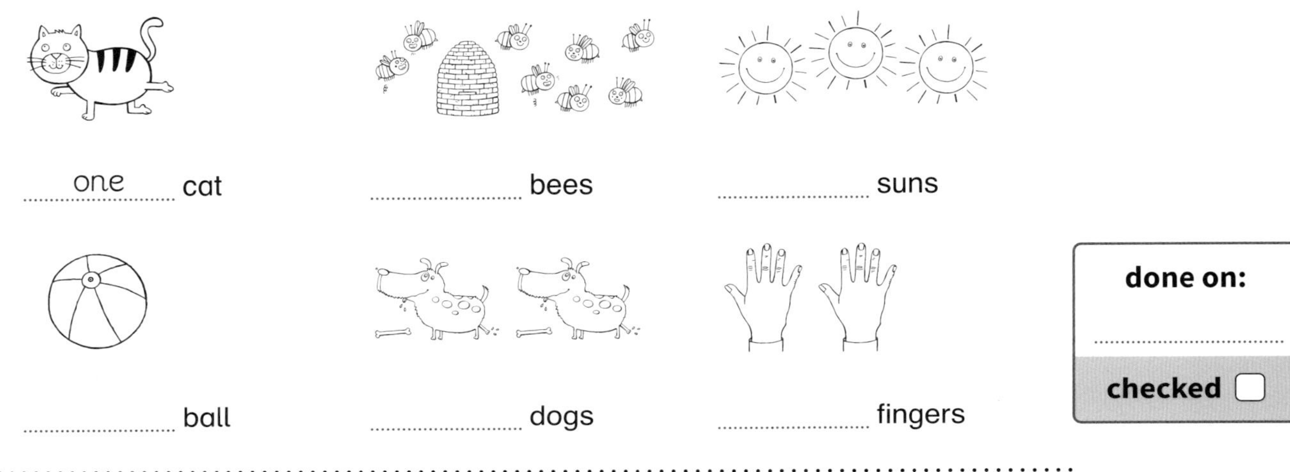


**done on:** ..........

**checked** ☐

**3. Circle.**

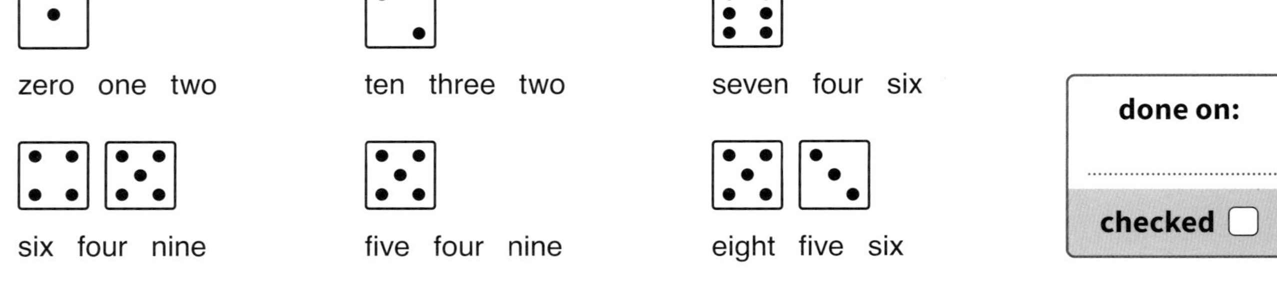


**done on:** ..........

**checked** ☐

**4. Write down the number words.**

0 ..........
1 ..........
2 ..........
3 ..........
4 ..........
5 ..........
6 ..........
7 ..........
8 ..........
9 ..........
10 ..........

**done on:** ..........

**checked** ☐

name: ..........................................

work schedule from .................... to ....................

**1. Draw lines.**

done on: ..................
checked ☐

**2. Find the number words. Circle.**

done on: ..................
checked ☐

**3. Write down the number words.**

| | | |
|---|---|---|
| noe .................... | svnee .................... | owt .................... |
| ixs .................... | net .................... | orfu .................... |
| nnie .................... | vfie .................... | roez .................... |

done on: ..................
checked ☐

**4. How much is it? Write.**

| | |
|---|---|
| three + six = .................... | eight – zero = .................... |
| one + two = .................... | ten – five = .................... |
| eight + two = .................... | seven – one = .................... |

done on: ..................
checked ☐

name: ..................................................

work schedule from .............................. to ..............................

**1. Read and colour.**

blue green red yellow orange pink

black grey white purple brown colourful

**done on:** ..............................
**checked** ☐

**2. Find the colour words. Circle.**

**done on:** ..............................
**checked** ☐

**3. Read and colour.**

a green apple

a black car

a brown cat

a purple present

a grey mouse

a red and blue ball

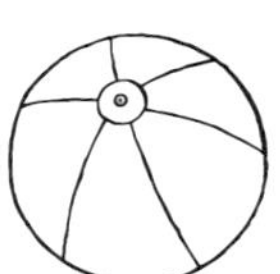

**done on:** ..............................
**checked** ☐

**4. Write down the English words.**

| | | |
|---|---|---|
| grün .............................. | rot .............................. | weiß .............................. |
| gelb .............................. | blau .............................. | braun .............................. |
| schwarz .............................. | orange .............................. | lila .............................. |

**done on:** ..............................
**checked** ☐

# colours



name: ..............................................................

work schedule from .............................. to ..............................

**1. Find 10 colour words. Circle.**

| H | R | E | D | Y | A | G | P |
|---|---|---|---|---|---|---|---|
| B | D | G | I | P | L | R | I |
| L | W | B | L | U | E | E | N |
| A | H | S | K | R | I | Y | K |
| C | I | L | O | P | R | X | V |
| K | T | Y | E | L | L | O | W |
| J | E | G | R | E | E | N | M |
| M | S | B | R | O | W | N | F |

**done on:** ..............................

**checked** ☐

**2. Colour the T-shirts.**

blue + red

purple + pink

green + grey

yellow + brown

**done on:** ..............................

**checked** ☐

**3. Fill in the right letters.**

| | | | |
|---|---|---|---|
| r ...... ...... | o r ...... ...... g ...... | b ...... ...... e | p ...... ...... p ...... ...... |
| ...... ...... l l ...... w | ...... o l ...... ...... r f ...... ...... | ...... h i ...... ...... | b ...... ...... ...... n |
| ...... r ...... e ...... | ...... ...... ...... k | g ...... e ...... | ...... l ...... c ...... |

**done on:** ..............................

**checked** ☐

**4. Read and colour.**

Nick's hair is brown.
Nick's pullover is blue.
Jenny's hair is red.
Jenny's T-shirt is green.
Billy's hair is black.
Billy's T-shirt is pink and purple.

**done on:** ..............................

**checked** ☐

© Verlag an der Ruhr | Autorinnen: Ricarda Dransmann, Svenja Sölter | ISBN 978-3-8346-4768-9 | www.verlagruhr.de | Illustrationen: © Anja Boretzki

# numbers & colours (mixed)

name: ..............................................................

work schedule from ........................ to ........................

## 1. Read and draw.

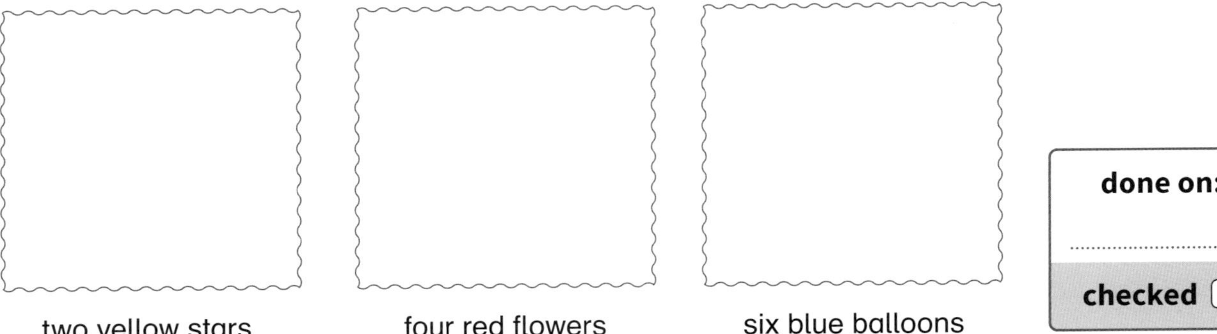

two yellow stars | four red flowers | six blue balloons

done on: ..............................

checked ☐

## 2. Colour the bird.

one = blue
two = red
three = green
four = pink
five = orange
six = yellow
seven = brown

done on: ..............................

checked ☐

## 3. What's missing? Write.

one, .............................., three, four, .............................. ,

six, .............................., eight, .............................. , ..............................

done on: ..............................

checked ☐

## 4. Right or wrong? Tick ✓ or ✗.

☐ There is one bird.

☐ There are three flowers.

☐ There are eight apples.

☐ There are six tomatoes.

done on: ..............................

checked ☐

# my body

page 1

name: ..................

work schedule from .................. to ..................

**1. Fill in the right words.**

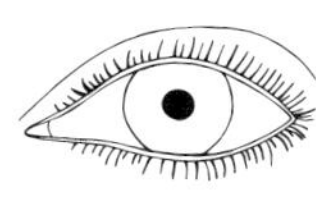
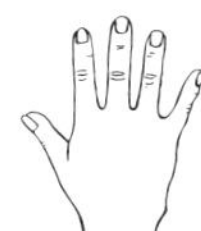
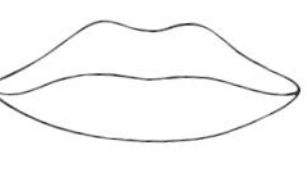

.................. .................. .................. .................. ..................

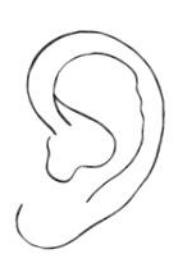

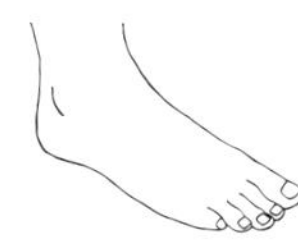
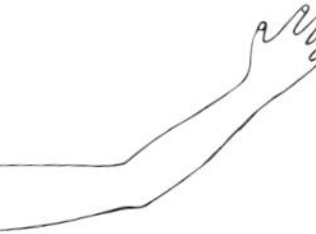

.................. .................. .................. ..................

eye hand head nose ear arm mouth leg foot

**done on:** ..................

**checked** ☐

**2. Find the body words. Circle.**

mouthhandeyeearnosefootheadlegarm

**done on:** ..................

**checked** ☐

**3. Do the crossword.**

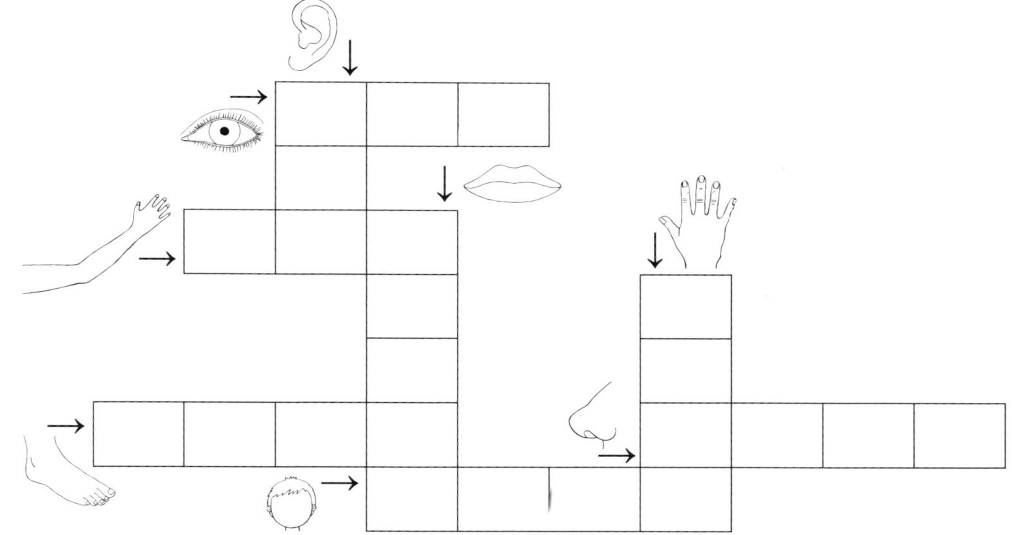

**done on:** ..................

**checked** ☐

**4. Complete the sentences.**

The monster has got three .................. .

The monster has got four .................. .

The monster has got five .................. .

**done on:** ..................

**checked** ☐

# my body

page 2

name: ..........

work schedule from .......... to ..........

**1. Tick the ✓ right box.**

☐ head
☐ ear
☐ foot

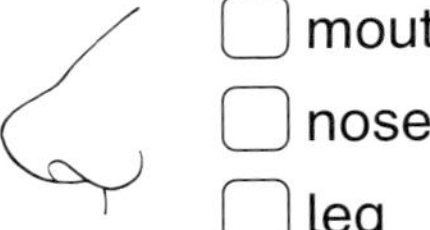

☐ mouth
☐ nose
☐ leg

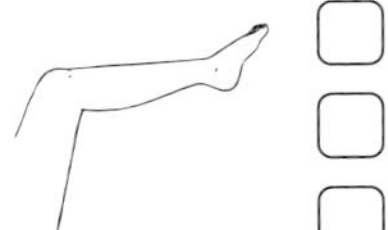

☐ head
☐ arm
☐ leg

☐ head
☐ leg
☐ mouth

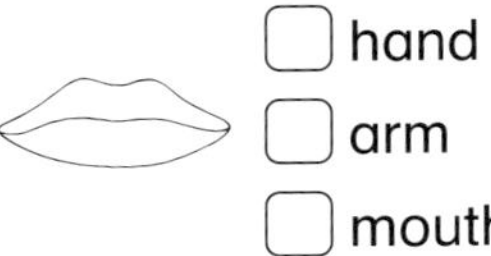

☐ hand
☐ arm
☐ mouth

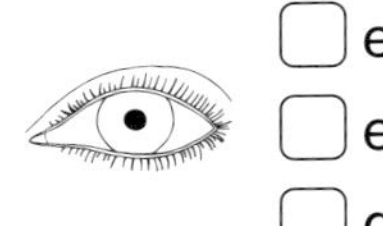

☐ ear
☐ eye
☐ arm

**done on:** ..........
**checked** ☐

**2. Find 9 body words. Circle.**

| | | | | | | | | |
|---|---|---|---|---|---|---|---|---|
| S | N | O | S | E | P | G | W | S |
| L | F | L | G | A | H | I | S | L |
| E | R | E | D | R | F | O | O | T |
| G | D | Y | L | P | W | A | H | B |
| W | H | E | A | D | R | C | V | A |
| R | C | K | M | O | U | T | H | R |
| H | A | N | D | J | K | V | E | M |

**done on:** ..........
**checked** ☐

**3. Count.**

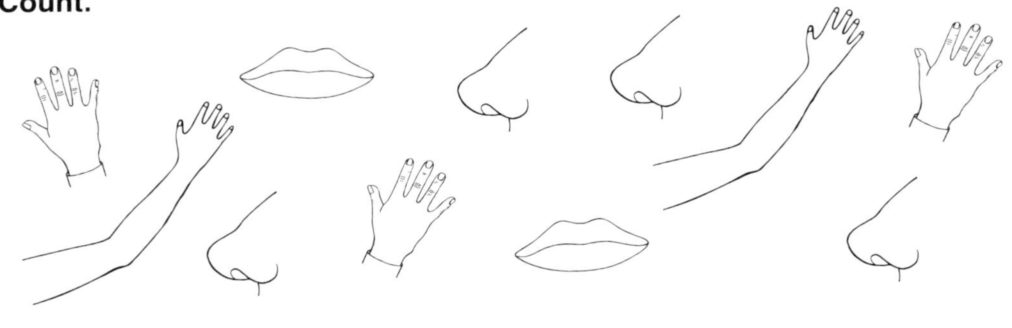

.......... hands .......... arms .......... noses .......... mouths

**done on:** ..........
**checked** ☐

**4. Do you know the body words? Write.**

yee .......... soen .......... nadh ..........

tofo .......... mar .......... egl ..........

thuom .......... aedh .......... era ..........

**done on:** ..........
**checked** ☐

# feelings

page 1

name: ..........................................

work schedule from .................... to ....................

**1. Fill in the right words.**

.................... .................... .................... ....................

.................... .................... .................... ....................

in love surprised hungry happy sad angry scared tired

**done on:** ..................

**checked** ☐

**2. Find 7 feeling words. Circle.**

| S | S | F | E | M | H | U | N | G | R | Y | U |
|---|---|---|---|---|---|---|---|---|---|---|---|
| C | F | G | E | N | A | H | K | Y | H | N | S |
| A | H | W | R | G | P | F | S | X | O | K | A |
| R | U | E | M | L | P | G | T | I | R | E | D |
| E | A | N | G | R | Y | A | G | P | B | H | N |
| D | G | S | U | R | P | R | I | S | E | D | M |

**done on:** ..................

**checked** ☐

**3. Find the odd one out.**

1) sad – bed – happy – tired

2) in love – angry – scared – hair

3) hungry – sad – tired – sun

4) hat – happy – angry – surprised

**done on:** ..................

**checked** ☐

**4. Read and draw the faces.**

happy

sad

angry

**done on:** ..................

**checked** ☐

name: ..............................

work schedule from .................... to ....................

**1. Tick ✓ the right box.**

Is Ali happy? Is Lilly sad? Is Milan angry?

☐ Yes, he is. ☐ Yes, she is. ☐ Yes, he is.
☐ No, he isn't. ☐ No, she isn't. ☐ No, he isn't.

**done on:** ..............
**checked** ☐

**2. Do the crosssword.**

**done on:** ..............
**checked** ☐

**3. Do you know the feeling words? Write.**

das .............................. yhapp .............................. gryna ..............................

iredt .............................. gnuhry .............................. carsed ..............................

**done on:** ..............
**checked** ☐

**4. How are you today? Draw and write.**

..............................................................

..............................................................

..............................................................

**done on:** ..............
**checked** ☐

name: ..........

work schedule from .......... to ..........

**1. Draw lines.**

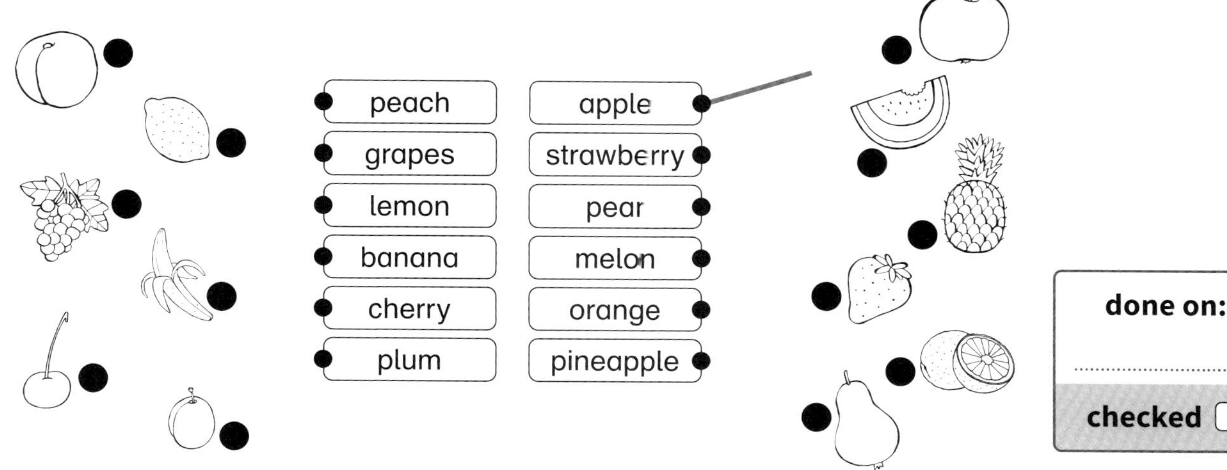


**done on:** ..........

**checked** ☐

**2. Do you know the fruit words? Write.**

onlem ..........

plepa ..........

rryech ..........

yberrawstr ..........

pppineale ..........

achpe ..........

**done on:** ..........

**checked** ☐

**3. Count.**

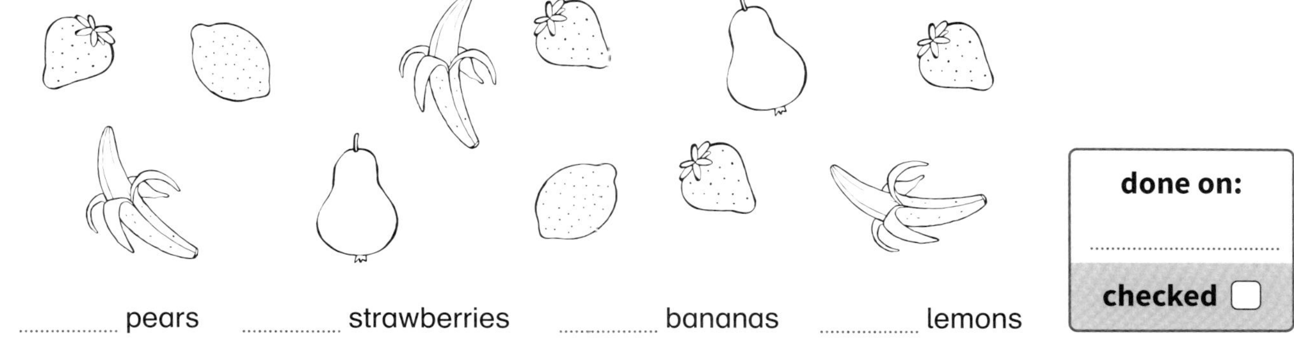

.......... pears .......... strawberries .......... bananas .......... lemons

**done on:** ..........

**checked** ☐

**4. What's in your fruit salad? Draw and write.**

In my fruit salad, there are

..........

..........

..........

..........

..........

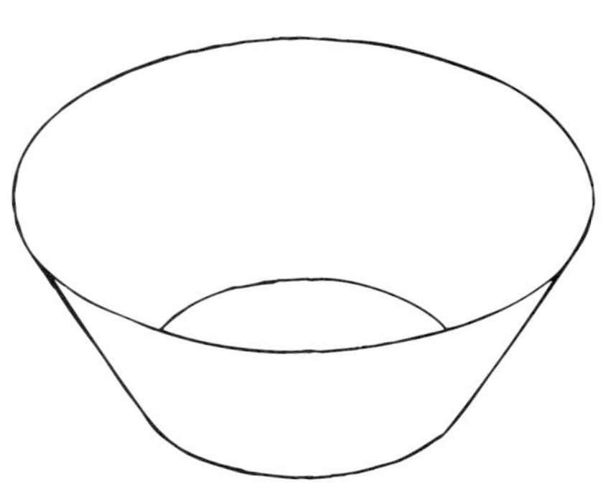

**done on:** ..........

**checked** ☐

name: ..........

work schedule from .......... to ..........

**1. Find the odd one out.**

1) cherry – pear – carrot – apple

2) banana – bread – lemon – peach

3) egg – strawberry – orange – melon

4) pineapple – apple – cherry – cheese

**done on:** ..........
**checked** ☐

**2. Read and draw.**

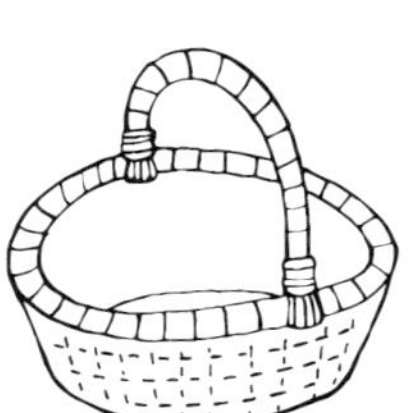

**done on:** ..........
**checked** ☐

**3. 2 fruits are in the basket. Do the labyrinth. Write.**

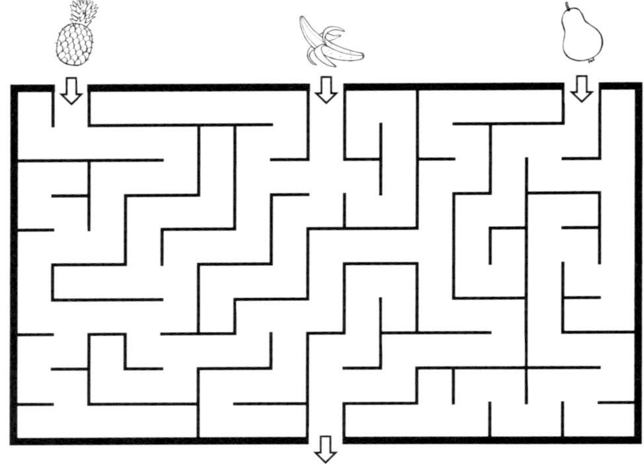

In the basket are a .......... and a .......... .

**done on:** ..........
**checked** ☐

**4. Write down the funny fruit names.**

apple + banana = applebanana

 + lemon = ..........

 + cherry = ..........

orange + pineapple = ..........

**done on:** ..........
**checked** ☐

# vegetables

page 1

name: ..........

work schedule from .......... to ..........

**1. Draw lines.**

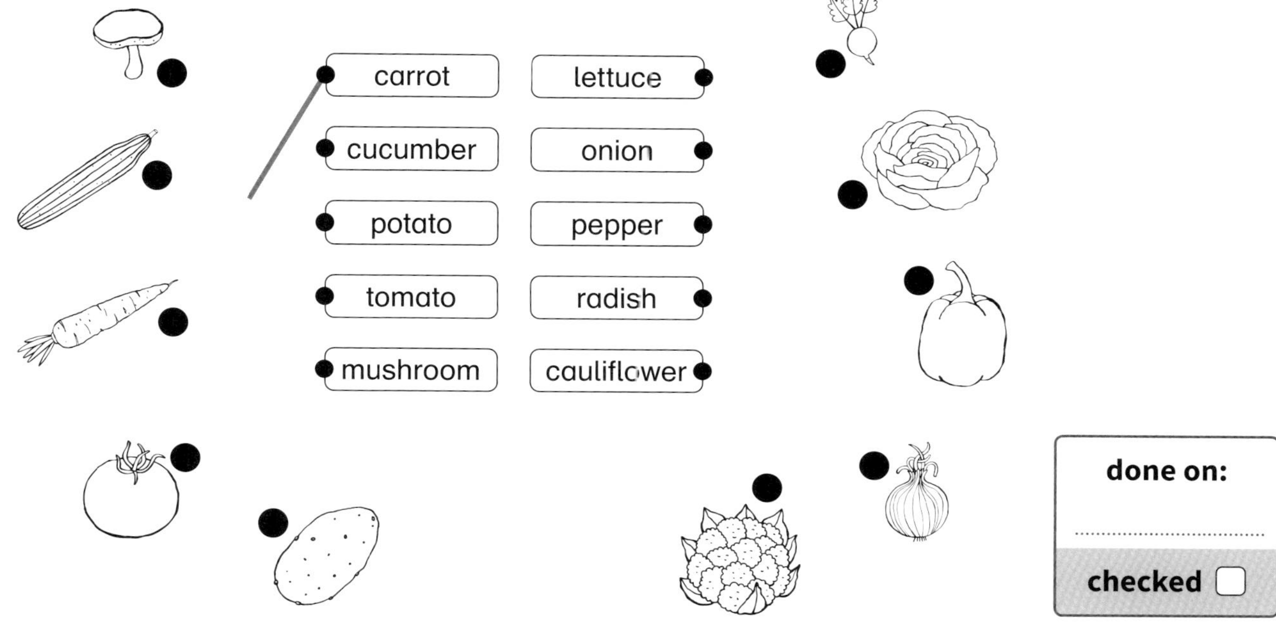


**done on:** ..........

**checked** ☐

**2. Find the odd one out.**

1) pie – cucumber – tomato – carrot

2) mushroom – onion – bee – potato

3) onion – radish – lettuce – fridge

4) pepper – pear – carrot – cauliflower

**done on:** ..........

**checked** ☐

**3. Read and draw.**

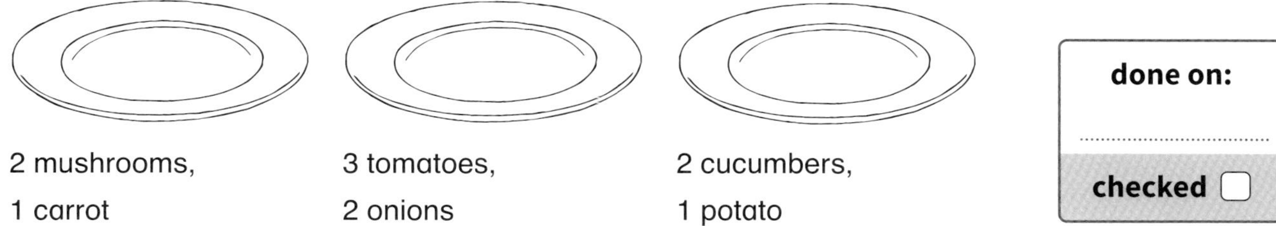

2 mushrooms,
1 carrot

3 tomatoes,
2 onions

2 cucumbers,
1 potato

**done on:** ..........

**checked** ☐

**4. Do you like …? Tick ✓ or ✗.**

… lettuce? ☐ … carrots? ☐ … mushrooms? ☐

… cauliflower? ☐ … tomatoes? ☐ … potatoes? ☐

**done on:** ..........

**checked** ☐

name: ..............................

work schedule from .................... to ....................

**1. Tick ✓ the right box.**

☐ mushroom
☐ lettuce
☐ pepper

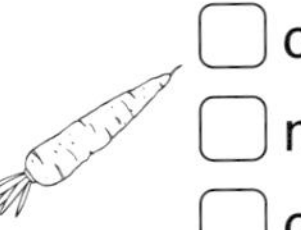

☐ cucumber
☐ mushroom
☐ carrot

☐ onion
☐ pepper
☐ radish

☐ potato
☐ onion
☐ tomato

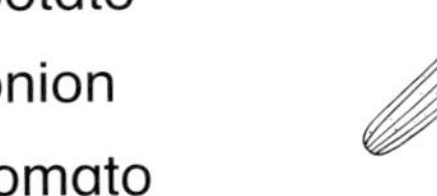

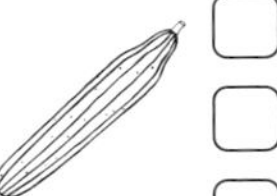

☐ carrot
☐ lettuce
☐ cucumber

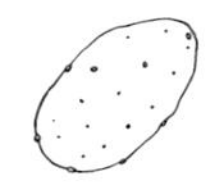

☐ cauliflower
☐ potato
☐ radish

**done on:** ..........

**checked** ☐

**2. Find 8 vegetable words. Circle.**

| | | | | | | | | | | | |
|---|---|---|---|---|---|---|---|---|---|---|---|
| P | O | T | A | T | O | M | B | R | C | S | L |
| T | I | R | K | T | O | W | R | B | A | A | E |
| O | R | A | U | P | E | P | P | E | R | O | T |
| M | A | D | N | R | D | I | S | F | R | B | T |
| A | O | I | Y | P | E | O | N | I | O | N | U |
| T | Z | S | U | E | W | R | S | N | T | W | C |
| O | S | H | M | U | S | H | R | O | O | M | E |

**done on:** ..........

**checked** ☐

**3. What's in your favourite vegetable meal? Write and draw.**

In my favourite vegetable meal there are

..............................

..............................

..............................

**done on:** ..........

**checked** ☐

**4. Look and write.**

| | 1 | 2 | 3 | 4 |
|---|---|---|---|---|
| **A** | | | | |
| **B** | | | | |
| **C** | | | | |

A1 radish

A2 ..............................

A3 ..............................

B3 ..............................

C3 ..............................

**done on:** ..........

**checked** ☐

# fruit & vegetables (mixed)

name: ..............................................................

work schedule from .............................. to ..............................

**1. Write down the fruit and vegetable words.**

fruit:

................ ..................................................

................ ..................................................

vegetable:

..................................................................

..................................................................

**done on:** ..............................

**checked** ☐

**2. Find the fruit and vegetable words. Circle.**

lettuceorangeradishonionmelontomatoapplepepperpeachpotato

**done on:** ..............................

**checked** ☐

**3. Write the names on the boxes.**

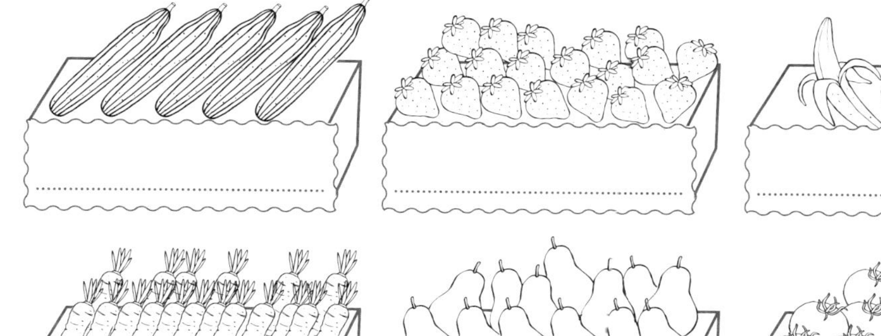

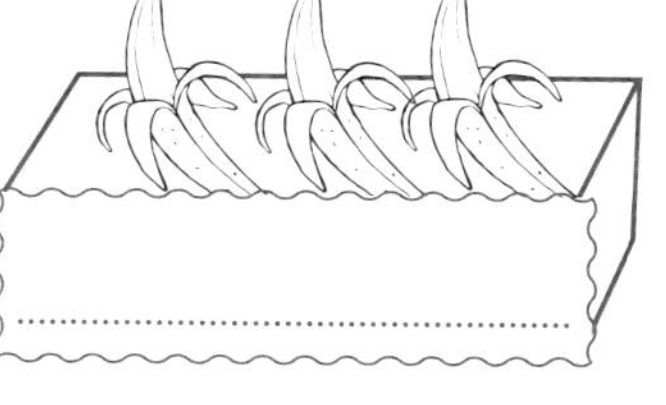

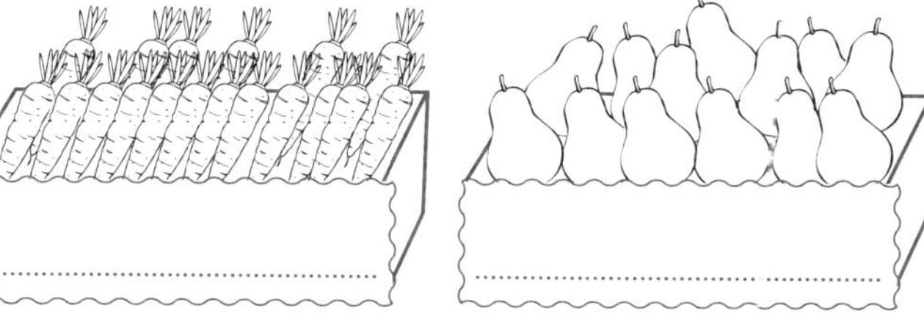

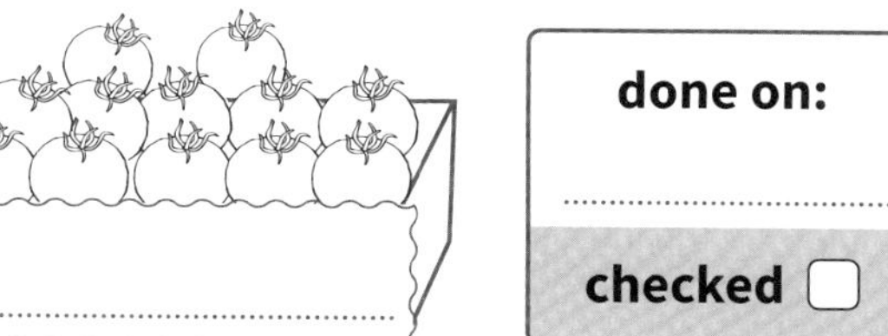

**done on:** ..............................

**checked** ☐

**4. Write down the English shopping list.**

**done on:** ..............................

**checked** ☐

name: ..............................

work schedule from .................. to ..................

**1. Draw lines.**

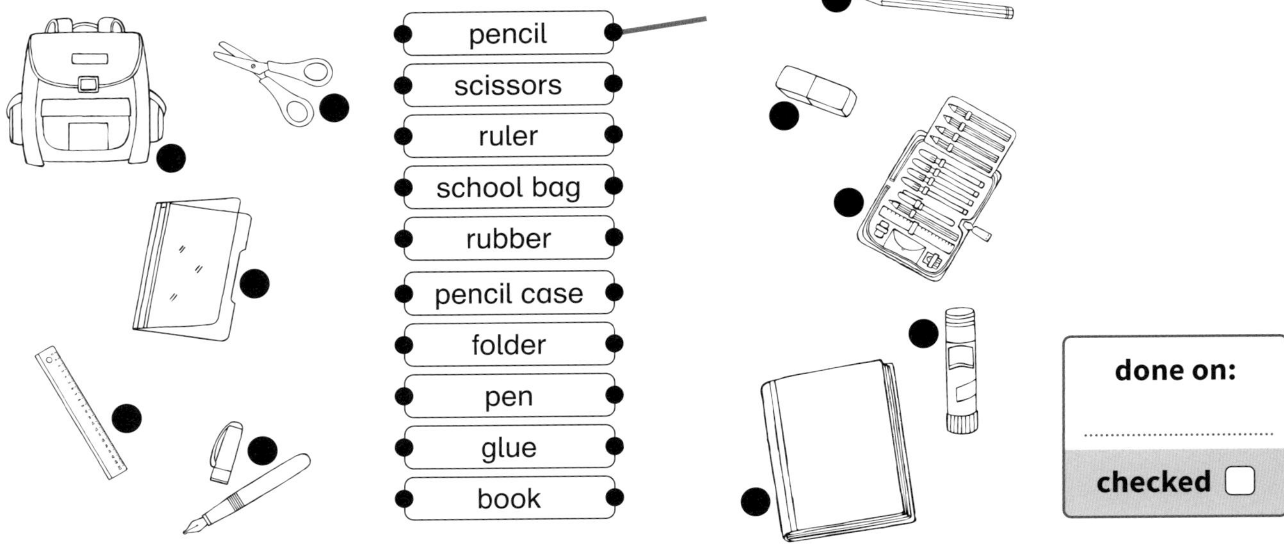


**done on:** ..................

**checked** ☐

**2. Tick ✓ the right box.**

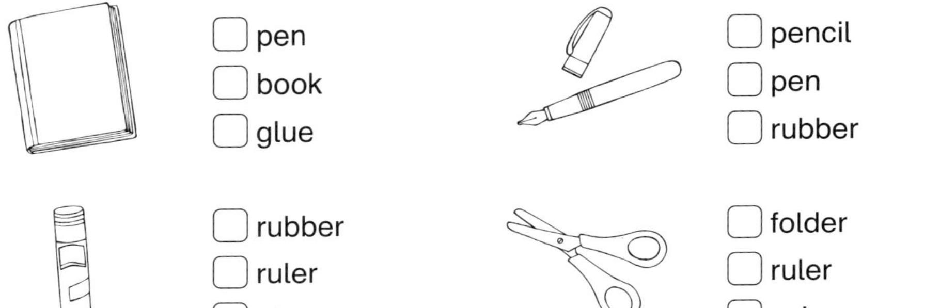


**done on:** ..................

**checked** ☐

**3. Fill in the right letters.**

b ..... ..... k    s ..... ..... o o .....    ..... ..... g    ..... u ..... b ..... .....    f ..... ..... d ..... .....

..... e .....    s ..... ..... s ..... ..... r .....    ..... e ..... c ..... .....    ..... l ..... e

**done on:** ..................

**checked** ☐

**4. What's in your school bag? Draw and write 4 things.**

In my schoolbag there are

..............................

..............................

..............................

..............................

**done on:** ..................

**checked** ☐

name: ..............................

work schedule from .................... to ....................

**1. Find the school words. Circle.**

scissorsrulerbookgluepencilrubberfolderpen

**done on:** ..................
**checked** ☐

**2. Look and write.**

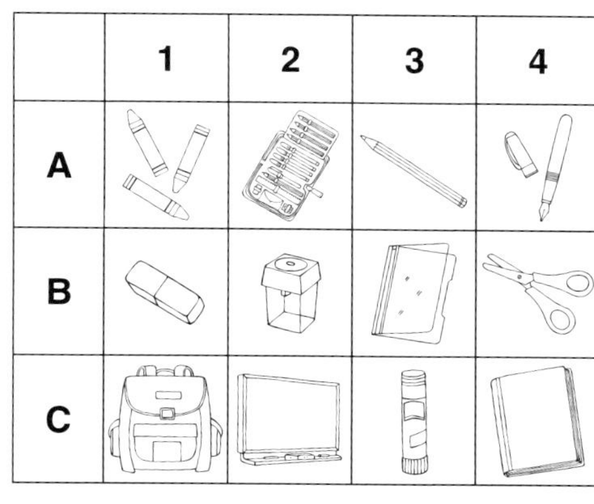

A3 pencil

A4 ..............................

B1 ..............................

B3 ..............................

C1 ..............................

C4 ..............................

**done on:** ..................
**checked** ☐

**3. Do the crossword.**

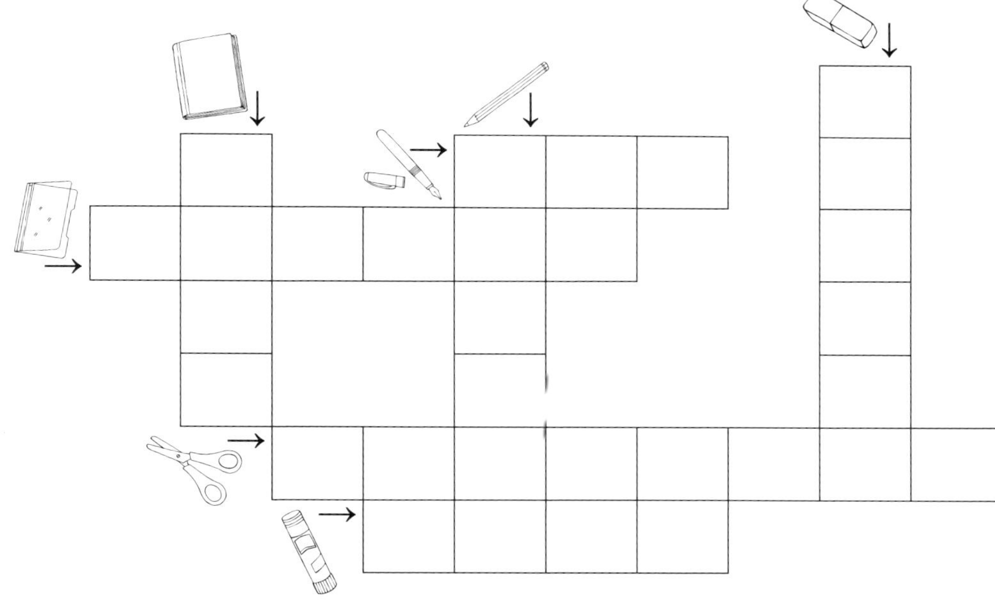

**done on:** ..................
**checked** ☐

**4. What's on the desk? Write.**

On the desk there are

..............................

..............................

..............................

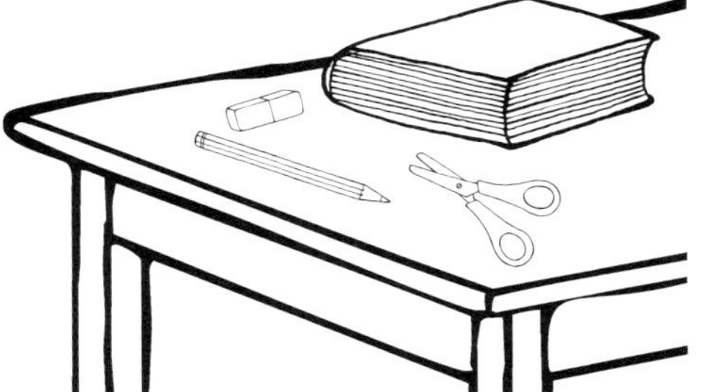

**done on:** ..................
**checked** ☐

© Verlag an der Ruhr | Autorinnen: Ricarda Dransmann, Svenja Sölter | ISBN 978-3-8346-4768-9 | www.verlagruhr.de | Illustrationen: © Anja Boretzki

# weather

**page 1**

name: ..............................

work schedule from .................... to ....................

**1. Fill in the right words.**

 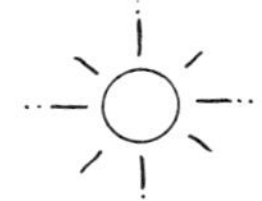  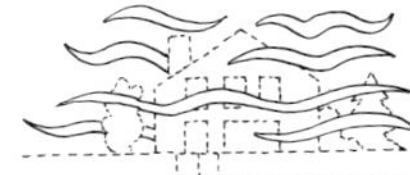

.................... .................... .................... ....................

.................... .................... ....................

foggy rainy thunder and lightning windy sunny snowy cloudy

**done on:** ....................

**checked** ☐

**2. Do you know the weather words? Write.**

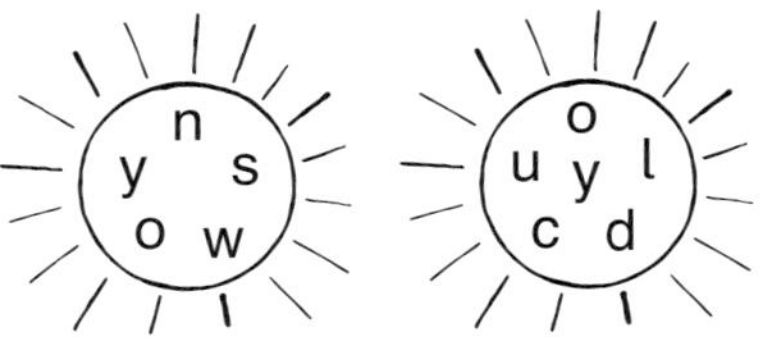


.................... .................... .................... .................... ....................

**done on:** ....................

**checked** ☐

**3. Find 6 weather words. Circle.**

| R | N | R | A | E | M | F | R | F | R | F |
|---|---|---|---|---|---|---|---|---|---|---|
| A | S | C | L | U | F | Y | F | G | V | O |
| I | N | S | U | N | N | Y | S | Y | O | G |
| N | O | N | R | L | S | Z | N | Y | U | G |
| Y | W | S | U | C | C | L | O | U | D | Y |
| R | Y | W | I | N | D | Y | R | I | N | F |

**done on:** ....................

**checked** ☐

**4. Read and draw.**

It's sunny. It's rainy. It's snowy. It's foggy.

**done on:** ....................

**checked** ☐

name: ..........

work schedule from .......... to ..........

**1. Fill in the right numbers.**

(1) sunny
(2) cloudy
(3) windy
(4) rainy
(5) foggy
(6) thunder and lightning
(7) snowy

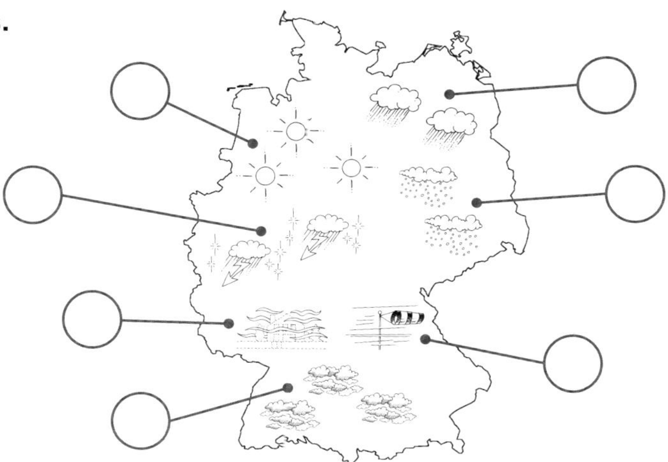

**done on:** ..........
**checked** ☐

**2. Find the odd one out.**

1) windy – sunny – happy – snowy

2) sunny – foggy – rainy – thirsty

3) funny – windy – snowy – cloudy

4) cloudy – rainy – sunny – silly

**done on:** ..........
**checked** ☐

**3. Fill in the right words.**

We go to the beach. It's .......... .

I can't see very much. It's .......... .

We build a snowman. It's .......... .

I need my umbrella. It's .......... .

We fly a kite. It's .......... .

snowy windy sunny rainy foggy

**done on:** ..........
**checked** ☐

**4. What's the weather like today? Draw and write.**

Today, it's

..........

..........

..........

**done on:** ..........
**checked** ☐

name: ...........................................

work schedule from .................... to ....................

**1. Put the days of the week in the right order.**

Thursday Monday Wednesday Tuesday Sunday Saturday Friday

1 ....................  2 ....................

3 ....................  4 ....................

5 ....................  6 ....................

7 ....................

**done on:** ....................

**checked** ☐

**2. Find 8 month words. Circle.**

| R | A | M | O | A | S | R | B | N | S |
|---|---|---|---|---|---|---|---|---|---|
| A | J | A | N | U | A | R | Y | E | J |
| U | R | R | E | C | P | W | O | S | U |
| G | N | C | P | N | R | F | D | D | N |
| U | M | H | R | A | I | N | A | F | E |
| S | A | C | J | U | L | Y | O | C | T |
| T | Y | D | E | C | E | M | B | E | R |

**done on:** ....................

**checked** ☐

**3. Fill in the right season.**

.................... .................... .................... ....................

spring summer autumn winter

**done on:** ....................

**checked** ☐

**4. Write about your birthday.**

My birthday is in this month: ....................

My birthday is in this season: ....................

This year, my birthday is on this day of the week: ....................

**done on:** ....................

**checked** ☐

name: ..............................

work schedule from .................. to ..................

**1. Fill in the right day of the week.**

October 5: ..............................

October 14: ..............................

October 24: ..............................

October 29: ..............................

OCTOBER 2021

| MON | TUE | WED | THU | FRI | SAT | SUN |
|---|---|---|---|---|---|---|
| | | | | 1 | 2 | 3 |
| 4 | 5 | 6 | 7 | 8 | 9 | 10 |
| 11 | 12 | 13 | 14 | 15 | 16 | 17 |
| 18 | 19 | 20 | 21 | 22 | 23 | 24 |
| 25 | 26 | 27 | 28 | 29 | 30 | 31 |

**done on:** ..................

**checked** ☐

**2. Fill in the right day of the week.**

Today is Monday. Tomorrow is .............................. .

Today is Sunday. Yesterday was .............................. .

Yesterday was Friday. Today is .............................. .

Tomorrow is Thursday. Today is .............................. .

**done on:** ..................

**checked** ☐

**3. Draw lines.**

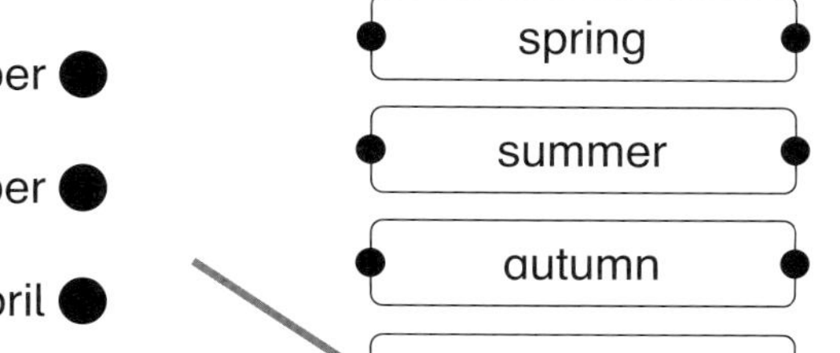

September ●
December ●
April ●
August ●

spring
summer
autumn
winter

● July
● February
● October
● March

**done on:** ..................

**checked** ☐

**4. What's your favourite season? Write and draw.**

My favourite season is

..............................

**done on:** ..................

**checked** ☐

# pets

page 1

name: ..........

work schedule from .......... to ..........

**1. Fill in the right words.**

.......... .......... .......... ..........

.......... .......... .......... ..........

cat dog tortoise rabbit fish mouse budgie hamster

**done on:** ..........

**checked** ☐

**2. Find 7 pet words. Circle.**

| M | T | O | R | T | O | I | S | E |
|---|---|---|---|---|---|---|---|---|
| O | W | S | F | I | H | K | I | S |
| U | F | B | U | D | G | I | E | C |
| S | I | F | L | O | F | S | G | A |
| E | S | G | D | G | G | L | J | T |
| A | H | A | M | S | T | E | R | K |

**done on:** ..........

**checked** ☐

**3. Fill in the right words.**

My pet can swim. It's a .......... .

My pet can fly. It is blue. It's a .......... .

My pet is black. It says "Miaow". It's a .......... .

My pet is green and very slow. It's a .......... .

**done on:** ..........

**checked** ☐

**4. Find the odd one out.**

1) cat – apple – dog – tortoise

2) dog – budgie – house – fish

3) rabbit – dog – fish – car

4) mouse – hamster – lolly – rabbit

**done on:** ..........

**checked** ☐

name: ..................................................

work schedule from .................... to ....................

**1. Tick ✓ the right box.**

☐ dog
☐ rabbit
☐ mouse

☐ cat
☐ rabbit
☐ hamster

☐ tortoise
☐ fish
☐ hamster

☐ budgie
☐ cat
☐ tortoise

**done on:** ..................
**checked** ☐

**2. Fill in the right letters.**

d ...... ......

...... a ...... s t ...... ......

...... ...... b ...... i t

...... o ...... s ......

b ...... d ...... ...... e

...... ...... r t ...... i ...... ......

**done on:** ..................
**checked** ☐

**3. Whose is it? Write.**

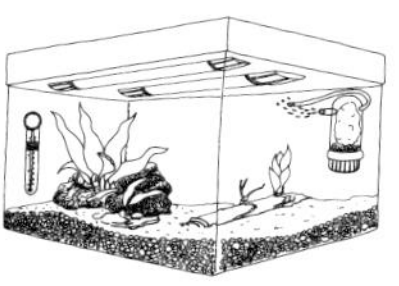

..................................

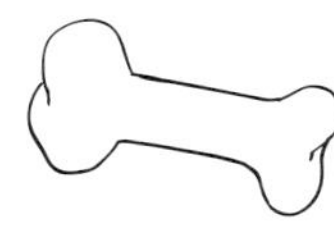

..................................

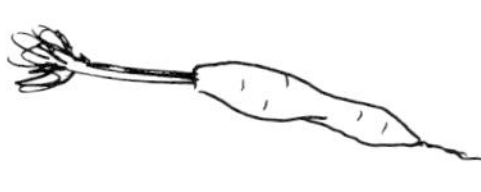

..................................

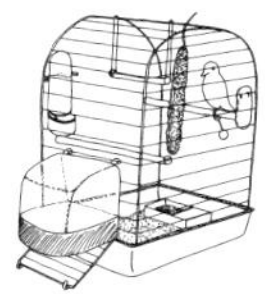

..................................

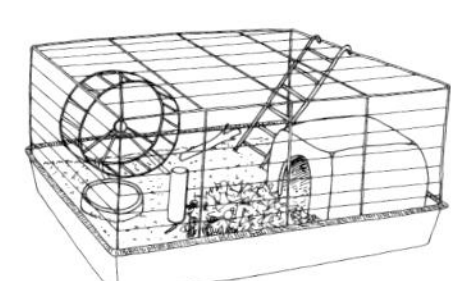

..................................

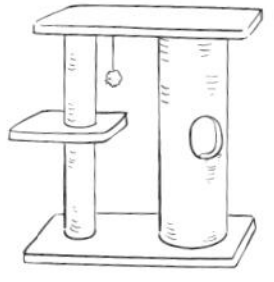

..................................

budgie hamster dog fish rabbit cat

**done on:** ..................
**checked** ☐

**4. What's your favourite pet? Write and draw.**

My favourite pet is a

.................................................. .

It is .................................... (colour).

It likes ..................................................

.................................................. (food).

**done on:** ..................
**checked** ☐

name: ..................................................

work schedule from .............................. to ..............................

**1. Draw lines.**

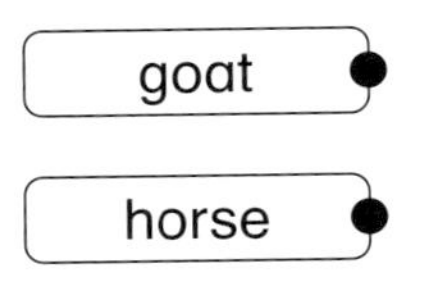

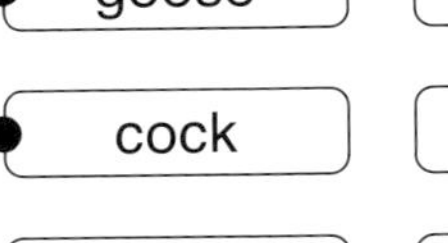

| | |
|---|---|
| sheep | goat |
| cow | horse |
| goose | pig |
| cock | duck |
| donkey | hen |

**done on:** ..............................

**checked** ☐

**2. Find the odd one out.**

1) cow – pig – sheep – blue

2) sheep – donkey – horse – house

3) duck – tiger – cow – goose

4) pig – cock – crocodile – horse

**done on:** ..............................

**checked** ☐

**3. Read and draw lines.**

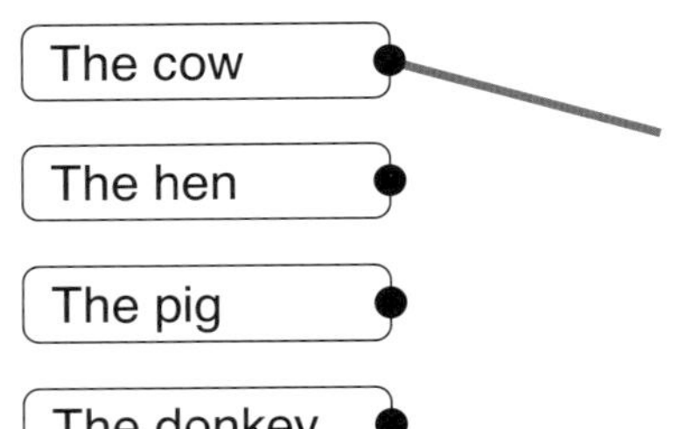

| | |
|---|---|
| The cow | is pink. |
| The hen | makes "i-ah". |
| The pig | is black and white. |
| The donkey | lays eggs. |

**done on:** ..............................

**checked** ☐

**4. Fill in the right letters.**

h ..... r ..... .....     ..... o n ..... ..... y     s ..... e e .....     d u ..... .....

g ..... a .....     c ..... ..... k     g ..... ..... s .....     ..... e .....

**done on:** ..............................

**checked** ☐

# farm animals

page 2

name: ..............................

work schedule from .................... to ....................

**1. Read and draw.**

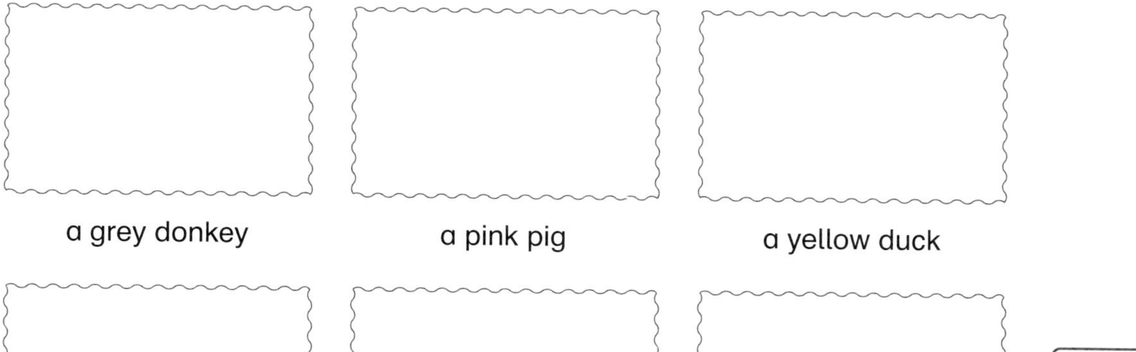

a grey donkey | a pink pig | a yellow duck

a brown horse | a white sheep | a colourful cock

**done on:** ....................

**checked** ☐

**2. Find the farm animal words. Circle.**

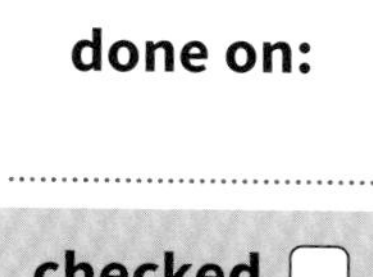

**done on:** ....................

**checked** ☐

**3. Find 10 farm animal words. Circle.**

| A | B | C | O | W | D | J | K | E | G | C |
|---|---|---|---|---|---|---|---|---|---|---|
| H | E | N | M | P | U | F | D | A | O | O |
| O | L | V | B | P | C | G | O | A | T | C |
| R | E | G | A | E | K | O | N | L | O | K |
| S | H | E | E | P | D | O | K | S | A | W |
| E | I | B | M | I | E | S | E | M | M | T |
| A | R | H | O | G | S | E | Y | B | O | Z |

**done on:** ....................

**checked** ☐

**4. Fill in the right words.**

It is pink and says “oink-oink”. It's a ....................................

It is big and gives milk. It's a ....................................

It lays eggs and says “cluck-cluck”. It's a ....................................

It is white, eats grass and says “baa-baa”. It's a ....................................

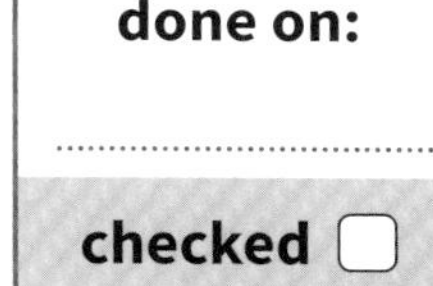

**done on:** ....................

**checked** ☐

# hobbies & sports

**page 1**

name: ..............................

work schedule from .............................. to ..............................

**1. Draw lines.**

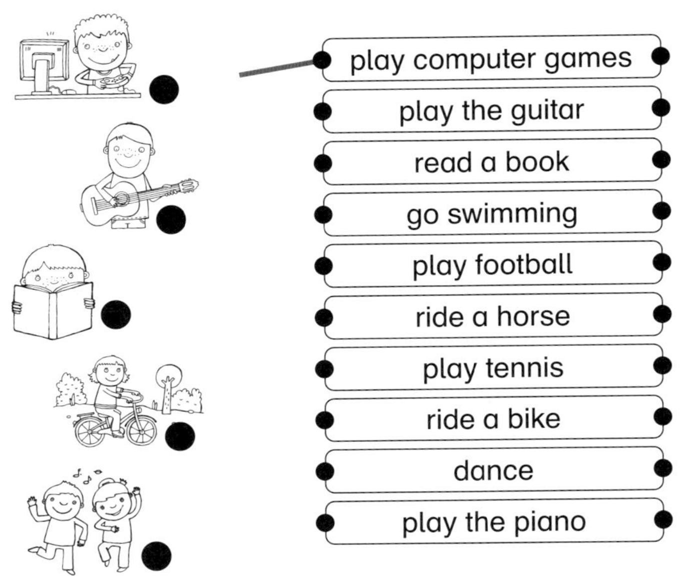

- play computer games
- play the guitar
- read a book
- go swimming
- play football
- ride a horse
- play tennis
- ride a bike
- dance
- play the piano

**done on:** ..............................

**checked** ☐

**2. Tick ✓ your answer.**

Do you like …

| | | |
|---|---|---|
| … to play football? | ☐ Yes, I do. | ☐ No, I don't. |
| … to read a book? | ☐ Yes, I do. | ☐ No, I don't. |
| … to play the piano? | ☐ Yes, I do. | ☐ No, I don't. |
| … to ride a horse? | ☐ Yes, I do. | ☐ No, I don't. |

**done on:** ..............................

**checked** ☐

**3. Guess the hobby. Read and write.**

For my hobby I need water, for example a pool or sea.

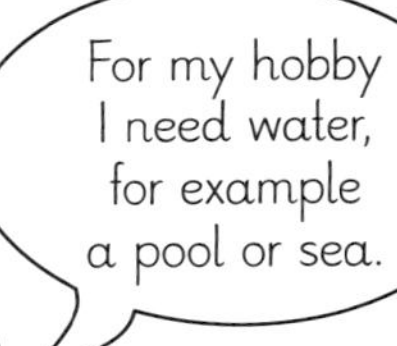

..............................

I can practice my hobby everywhere. I only need a book.

..............................

I need a ball for my hobby. I hit the ball with my feet.

..............................

**done on:** ..............................

**checked** ☐

**4. What's your favourite hobby? Write.**

My favourite hobby is ..............................

.............................................................................

**done on:** ..............................

**checked** ☐

name: ..............................

work schedule from .................... to ....................

**1. Tick ✓ the right box.**

- ☐ play football
- ☐ play tennis
- ☐ play the piano

- ☐ play computer games
- ☐ play tennis
- ☐ play the guitar

- ☐ go swimming
- ☐ read a book
- ☐ ride a bike

- ☐ dance
- ☐ ride a bike
- ☐ ride a horse

**done on:** ..............................
**checked** ☐

**2. What hobby is it? Look and write.**

A1 play tennis

A2 ..............................

B1 ..............................

B3 ..............................

C1 ..............................

C4 ..............................

**done on:** ..............................
**checked** ☐

**3. Tick ✓ your answer.**

Can you …

| | | |
|---|---|---|
| … play tennis? | ☐ Yes, I can. | ☐ No, I can't. |
| … play the guitar? | ☐ Yes, I can. | ☐ No, I can't. |
| … ride a bike? | ☐ Yes, I can. | ☐ No, I can't. |
| … dance? | ☐ Yes, I can. | ☐ No, I can't. |

**done on:** ..............................
**checked** ☐

**4. Right or wrong? Tick ✓ or ✗.**

- ☐ A boy is playing football.
- ☐ Two kids are swimming.
- ☐ A girl is playing tennis.
- ☐ Two kids are dancing.
- ☐ A boy is playing the guitar.
- ☐ Two kids are riding a bike.

**done on:** ..............................
**checked** ☐

name: ..............................................................

work schedule from ........................ to ........................

**1. Fill in the right words.**

.............................. .............................. .............................. ..............................

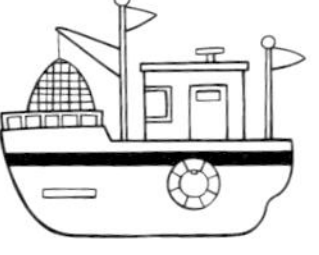

.............................. .............................. .............................. ..............................

.............................. .............................. .............................. ..............................

motorbike bus bike train car truck ship tram
underground taxi helicopter plane

**done on:** ..............................
**checked** ☐

**2. Find the vehicle words. Circle.**

taxiundergroundshiphelicoptermotorbiketraincarbikebusplanetruck

**done on:** ..............................
**checked** ☐

**3. Find the odd one out.**

1) ship – motorbike – guitar – underground

2) taxi – truck – pear – car

3) yellow – tram – plane – bike

4) bus – helicopter – taxi – eleven

**done on:** ..............................
**checked** ☐

**4. Do you know the vehicle words? Write.**

kibe .............................. rac .............................. xtai ..............................

nelpa .............................. cturk .............................. mrat ..............................

**done on:** ..............................
**checked** ☐

name: ..................................................

work schedule from .................... to ....................

## 1. Read and draw.

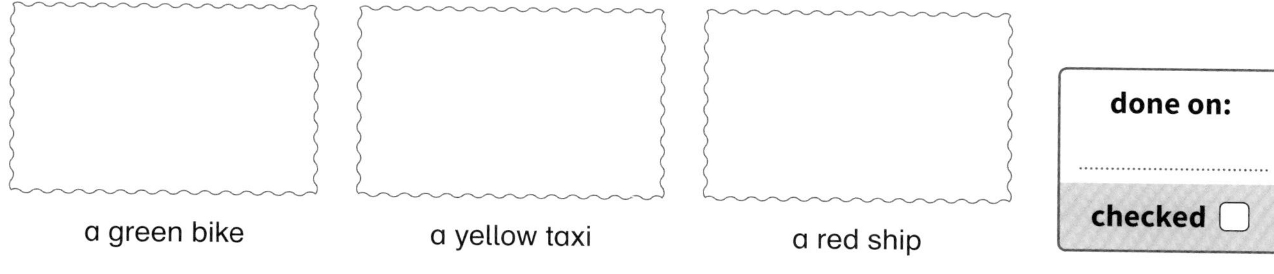

a green bike | a yellow taxi | a red ship

**done on:** ..................
**checked** ☐

## 2. Right or wrong? Tick ✓ or ✗.

☐ Anna goes to school by bike.

☐ Grandma travels by train.

☐ Sally goes to school by bus.

☐ Jim goes to work by car.

**done on:** ..................
**checked** ☐

## 3. Find 9 vehicle words. Circle.

| | | | | | | | | | | |
|---|---|---|---|---|---|---|---|---|---|---|
| U | N | D | E | R | G | R | O | U | N | D |
| L | O | P | L | A | N | E | S | K | S | T |
| T | A | Y | I | L | G | L | H | Y | O | R |
| R | A | T | C | A | R | T | B | U | S | U |
| A | U | R | O | B | I | L | I | X | H | C |
| I | F | A | P | T | A | X | I | L | I | K |
| N | L | M | I | K | E | W | T | W | P | C |

**done on:** ..................
**checked** ☐

## 4. How do you go to school? Write and draw.

I go to school by

..................................................

..................................................

**done on:** ..................
**checked** ☐

# my family

page 1

name: ..................................................

work schedule from .............................. to ..............................

**1. Draw lines.**

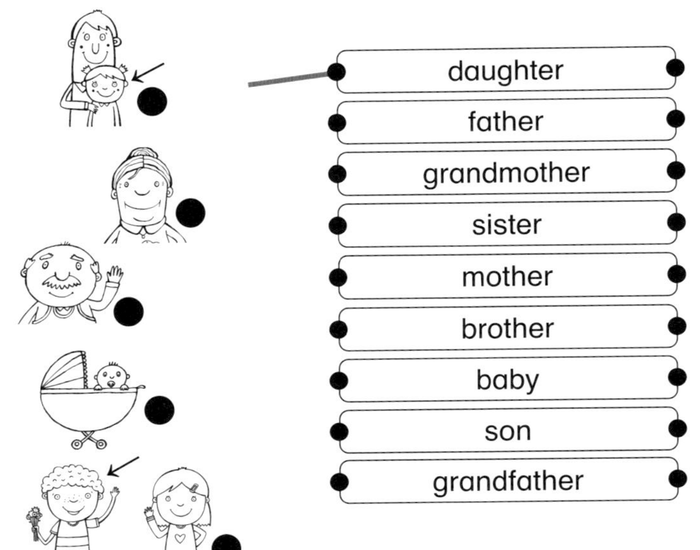

**done on:** ..............................

**checked** ☐

**2. Do you know the family words? Write.**

nos ..............................

fthera ..............................

bbya ..............................

serist ..............................

dghtaure ..............................

ohtrem ..............................

**done on:** ..............................

**checked** ☐

**3. Find 7 family words. Circle.**

| M | O | T | H | E | R | M | B | R | T | B |
|---|---|---|---|---|---|---|---|---|---|---|
| H | S | F | M | C | A | R | M | O | T | R |
| I | I | A | T | L | B | R | S | O | N | O |
| X | S | T | H | U | B | A | B | Y | Z | T |
| C | T | H | R | M | O | N | A | E | I | H |
| M | E | E | D | I | B | O | R | W | L | E |
| U | R | R | D | A | U | G | H | T | E | R |

**done on:** ..............................

**checked** ☐

**4. Fill in the right letters.**

b r ...... ...... h ...... r

d ...... ...... g h ...... e ......

m ...... t h ...... ......

...... i s ...... e ......

...... a ...... h ...... r

s ...... ......

**done on:** ..............................

**checked** 

name: ..............................

work schedule from .................. to ..................

**1. Draw lines.**

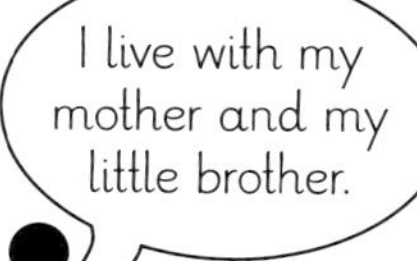

done on: ..............

checked ☐

**2. Find the family words. Circle.**

done on: ..............

checked ☐

**3. This is Mia's family tree. Who is it? Write.**

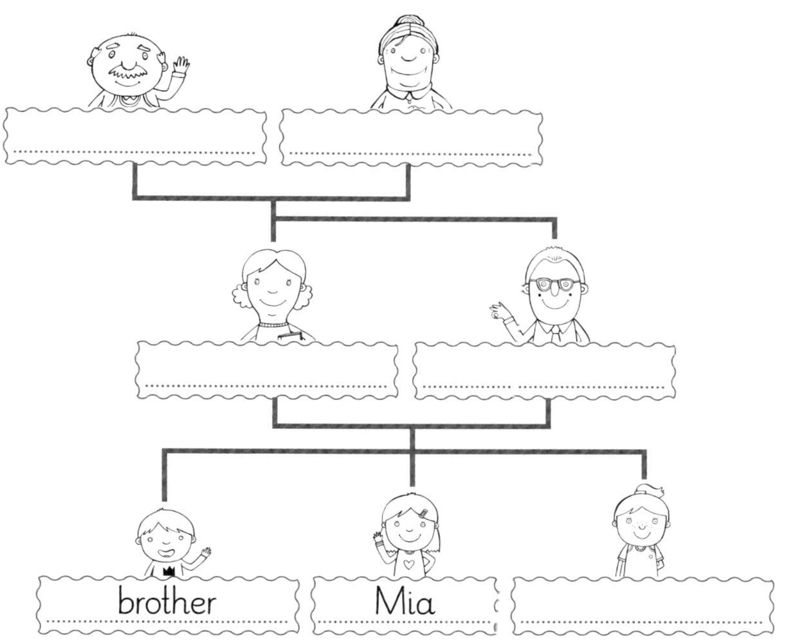


done on: ..............

checked ☐

**4. Who do you live with? Draw and write.**

I live with ..............................

..............................

..............................

done on: ..............

checked ☐

© Verlag an der Ruhr | Autorinnen: Ricarda Dransmann, Svenja Sölter | ISBN 978-3-8346-4768-9 | www.verlagruhr.de | Illustrationen: © Anja Boretzki

name: ........................................

work schedule from .................... to ....................

**1. Draw lines.**

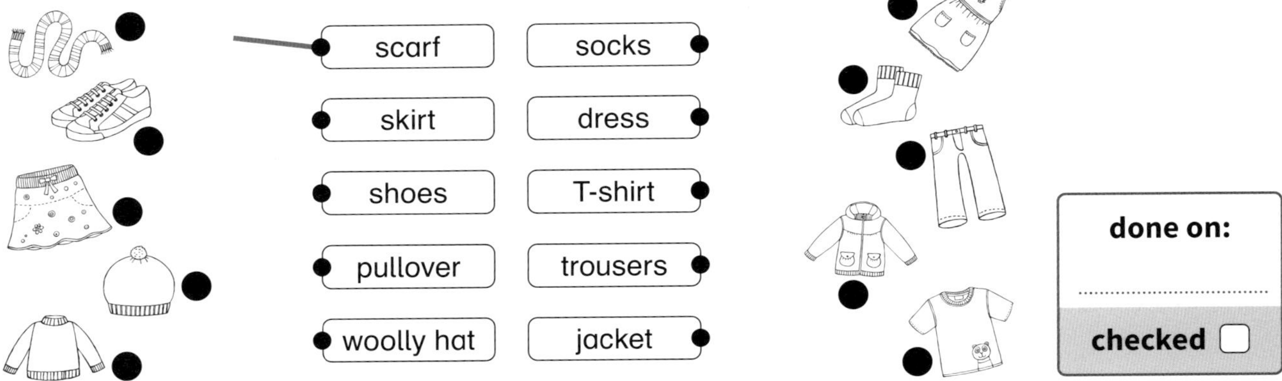


**2. Read and colour.**

Tilda's jacket is red.
Her trousers are blue.
Tilda has got a pink and purple woolly hat.
Tilda's scarf is grey.

done on: ....................
checked ☐

**3. Tick ✓ the right box.**

done on: ....................
checked ☐

**4. Look and write.**

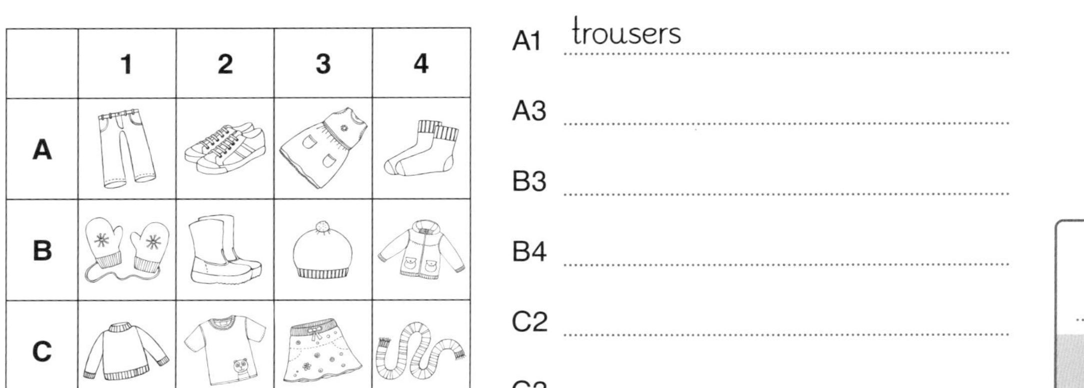

| | 1 | 2 | 3 | 4 |
|---|---|---|---|---|
| A | | | | |
| B | | | | |
| C | | | | |

A1 trousers

A3 ....................

B3 ....................

B4 ....................

C2 ....................

C3 ....................

done on: ....................
checked ☐

name: ..............................

work schedule from .................. to ..................

**1. Find 7 clothes words. Circle.**

| R | T | S | C | A | R | F | T | I | R | B |
|---|---|---|---|---|---|---|---|---|---|---|
| H | T | O | C | X | T | I | R | F | S | D |
| J | A | C | K | E | T | V | D | R | S | O |
| H | A | K | I | K | S | H | R | B | K | K |
| P | K | S | H | O | E | S | E | U | I | S |
| D | R | S | E | T | R | O | S | K | R | N |
| T | R | O | U | S | E | R | S | Y | T | O |

**done on:** ..................
**checked** ☐

**2. Right or wrong? Tick ✓ or ✗.**

☐ Ella is wearing shoes.
☐ Ella is wearing a skirt.
☐ Ella is wearing a woolly hat.
☐ Ella is wearing a pullover.
☐ Ella is wearing trousers.

**done on:** ..................
**checked** ☐

**3. Read and draw.**

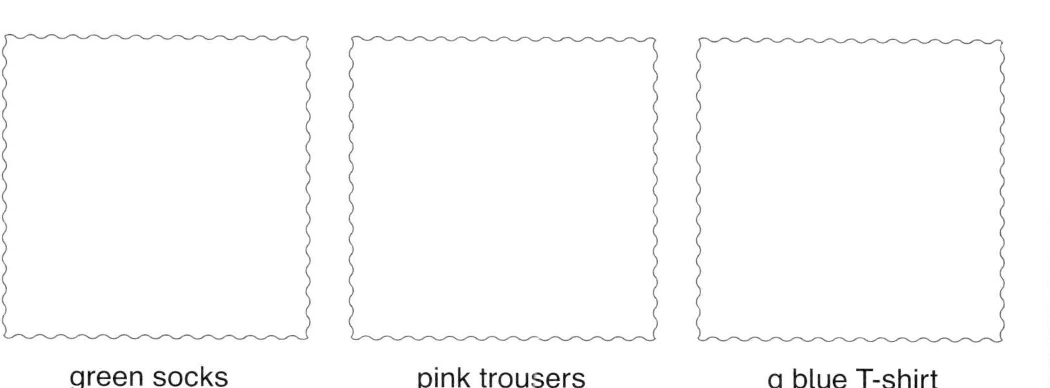

green socks | pink trousers | a blue T-shirt

**done on:** ..................
**checked** ☐

**4. What are your favourite clothes? Write and draw.**

My favourite clothes are

..............................

..............................

..............................

**done on:** ..................
**checked** ☐

# shopping

page 1

name: ..................................................

work schedule from .............................. to ..............................

**1. Draw lines.**

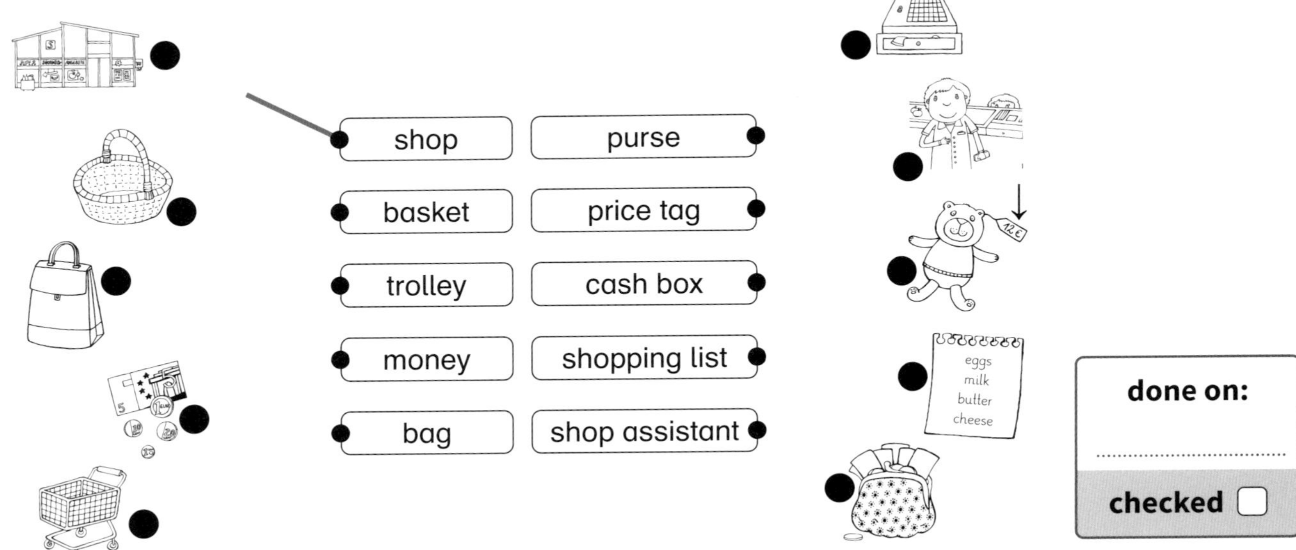


**done on:** ..............................

**checked** ☐

**2. Find the odd one out.**

1) shop – trolley – duck – money

2) price tag – basket – red – bag

3) cash box – shop assistant – farm – money

4) purse – cat – shopping list – trolley

**done on:** ..............................

**checked** ☐

**3. Find 8 shopping words. Circle.**

| P | R | I | C | E | T | A | G | Y | T | A | L | B |
|---|---|---|---|---|---|---|---|---|---|---|---|---|
| U | H | P | O | A | T | R | O | L | L | E | Y | A |
| R | B | S | J | S | N | C | S | R | O | H | P | S |
| S | A | T | D | H | E | T | M | U | P | U | R | K |
| E | G | H | M | O | N | E | Y | R | L | E | Y | E |
| M | S | H | O | P | P | I | N | G | L | I | S | T |

**done on:** ..............................

**checked** ☐

**4. Find the shopping words. Circle.**

shopbaskettrolleybagmoneypurseshopassistant

**done on:** ..............................

**checked** ☐

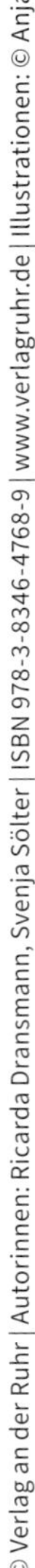

name: ..................................................

work schedule from .............................. to ..............................

**1. Read and draw.**

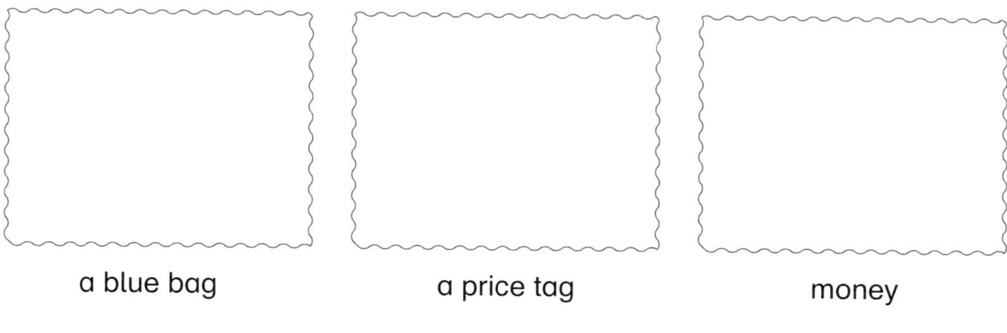

a blue bag | a price tag | money

a red purse | a cash box | a shop

**done on:** ..............................
**checked** ☐

**2. Fill in the right letters.**

p ...... ...... s ......  ...... a s ......  b ...... ......  ...... ...... ...... l l ...... ......  ...... h ...... ......

...... ...... n ...... y  p ...... ...... c ......  t ...... ......  b ...... ...... k ...... t  ...... ...... g

**done on:** ..............................
**checked** ☐

**3. Read the dialogue. Find the correct order and number.**

☐ Here you are. Good bye.
☐ Yes, it's perfect. How much is it?
☐ It's 20 pounds.
☐ Thank you. Good bye.
1 Hello. Can I help you?
☐ Hello. I'd like a new T-shirt.
☐ Do you like the blue T-shirt?

**done on:** ..............................
**checked** ☐

**4. Right or wrong? Tick ✓ or ✗.**

☐ There is a purse.
☐ There is some money.
☐ There is a trolley.
☐ There is a shop assistant.
☐ There is a woman with two bags.
☐ There is a price tag.

**done on:** ..............................
**checked** ☐

name: ..................................................

work schedule from .............................. to ..............................

**1. Draw lines.**

It's half past one.
It's eleven o'clock.
It's a quarter to ten.
It's half past nine.
It's a quarter past twelve.
It's seven o'clock.

**done on:** ..................
**checked** ☐

**2. Read and draw.**

It's two o'clock.

It's five o'clock.

It's twelve o'clock.

It's half past three.

It's a quarter past six.

It's a quarter to seven.

**done on:** ..................
**checked** ☐

**3. What time is it? Look and write.**

| | 1 | 2 | 3 | 4 |
|---|---|---|---|---|
| A | | | | |
| B | | | | |
| C | | | | |

A1 It's a quarter past twelve.

A3 ..................................................

B1 ..................................................

B4 ..................................................

C1 ..................................................

C4 ..................................................

**done on:** ..................
**checked** ☐

**4. Answer the questions.**

When do you get up? I get up at ..................................................

When do you go to school? I go to school at ..................................................

When do you have lunch? I have lunch at ..................................................

When do you go to bed? I go to bed at ..................................................

**done on:** ..................
**checked** ☐

# the time

page 2

name: ..............................

work schedule from .................. to ..................

**1. Tick ✓ the right answer.**

☐ It's four o'clock.
☐ It's five o'clock.
☐ It's three o'clock.

☐ It's half past six.
☐ It's half past eight.
☐ It's half past seven.

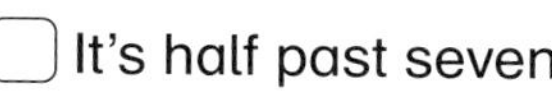

☐ It's a quarter to three.
☐ It's a quarter past three.
☐ It's a quarter past four.

☐ It's a quarter to eight.
☐ It's a quarter past nine.
☐ It's a quarter to nine.

**done on:** ..................
**checked** ☐

**2. What time is it? Write.**

6:00

It's .................................... .

9:30

It's .................................... .

8:15

It's .................................... .

2:45

It's .................................... .

**done on:** ..................
**checked** ☐

**3. Read. Tick ✓ the right box.**

I go to school at eight o'clock. ☐ 9:00 ☐ 8:00 ☐ 8:30

I get up at a quarter to seven. ☐ 6:45 ☐ 6:30 ☐ 7:00

I have lunch at half past twelve. ☐ 11:30 ☐ 12:30 ☐ 12:00

**done on:** ..................
**checked** ☐

**4. What time is it? Read and write.**

two o'clock + two hours = ..............................

six o'clock + 15 minutes = ..............................

seven o'clock + 30 minutes = ..............................

ten o'clock + 1 hour and 45 minutes = ..............................

**done on:** ..................
**checked** ☐

# Christmas

name: ..............................

work schedule from .................... to ....................

**1. Fill in the right words.**

.................... .................... ....................

.................... .................... ....................

snowman reindeer Santa Claus present angel Christmas tree

**done on:** ..........

**checked** ☐

**2. Read and draw.**

a green Christmas tree a brown reindeer a white snowman

**done on:** ..........

**checked** ☐

**3. Read and colour.**

The Christmas tree is green.
The Christmas balls are red, blue and orange.
The stars are yellow.
The presents are pink, purple and green.

**done on:** ..........

**checked** ☐

**4. Write a wish list for Santa Claus.**

Dear Santa Claus,

this year I wish for ..............................

..............................

..............................

**done on:** ..........

**checked** ☐

© Verlag an der Ruhr | Autorinnen: Ricarda Dransmann, Svenja Sölter | ISBN 978-3-8346-4768-9 | www.verlagruhr.de | Illustrationen: © Anja Boretzki

# Easter

name: ........................................

work schedule from .................... to ....................

**1. Fill in the right words.**

.................... .................... ....................

.................... .................... ....................

hen grass Easter egg nest Easter bunny chick

**done on:** ....................

**checked** ☐

**2. Find the Easter words. Circle.**

EasterbunnygrassnesthenEastereggchick

**done on:** ....................

**checked** ☐

**3. Find 6 Easter words. Circle.**

| E | A | S | T | E | R | B | U | N | N | Y |
|---|---|---|---|---|---|---|---|---|---|---|
| A | C | H | I | C | K | I | F | G | F | E |
| T | L | E | A | S | L | A | T | D | N | A |
| S | J | N | Y | G | E | A | H | S | E | T |
| B | W | E | B | R | J | B | L | T | S | R |
| F | A | S | N | A | Y | M | K | E | T | S |
| E | Y | E | A | S | T | E | R | E | G | G |
| G | E | R | A | S | D | C | I | C | K | D |

**done on:** ....................

**checked** ☐

**4. Read and draw.**

There is green grass.
There is the Easter bunny.
I can see three nests with lots of Easter eggs.
Two Easter eggs are red.
Three Easter eggs are blue.

**done on:** ....................

**checked** ☐

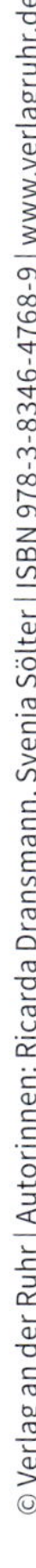

# LÖSUNGEN

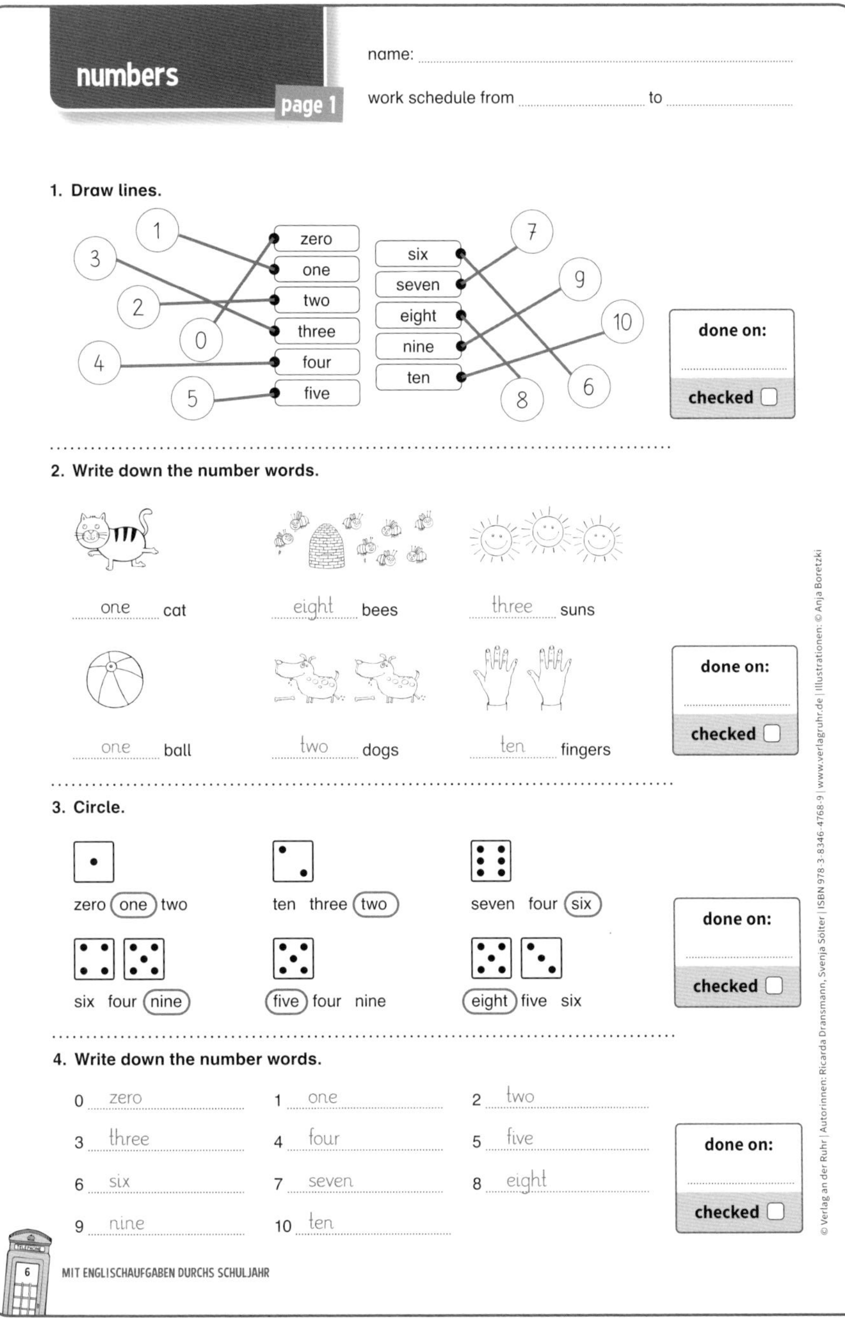
numbers page 1

name: ...

work schedule from ... to ...

1. Draw lines.

zero · one · two · three · four · five · six · seven · eight · nine · ten

done on: ... checked

2. Write down the number words.

one cat · eight bees · three suns

one ball · two dogs · ten fingers

done on: ... checked

3. Circle.

zero (one) two · ten three (two) · seven four (six)

six four (nine) · (five) four nine · (eight) five six

done on: ... checked

4. Write down the number words.

0 zero · 1 one · 2 two

3 three · 4 four · 5 five

6 six · 7 seven · 8 eight

9 nine · 10 ten

done on: ... checked



6 MIT ENGLISCHAUFGABEN DURCHS SCHULJAHR

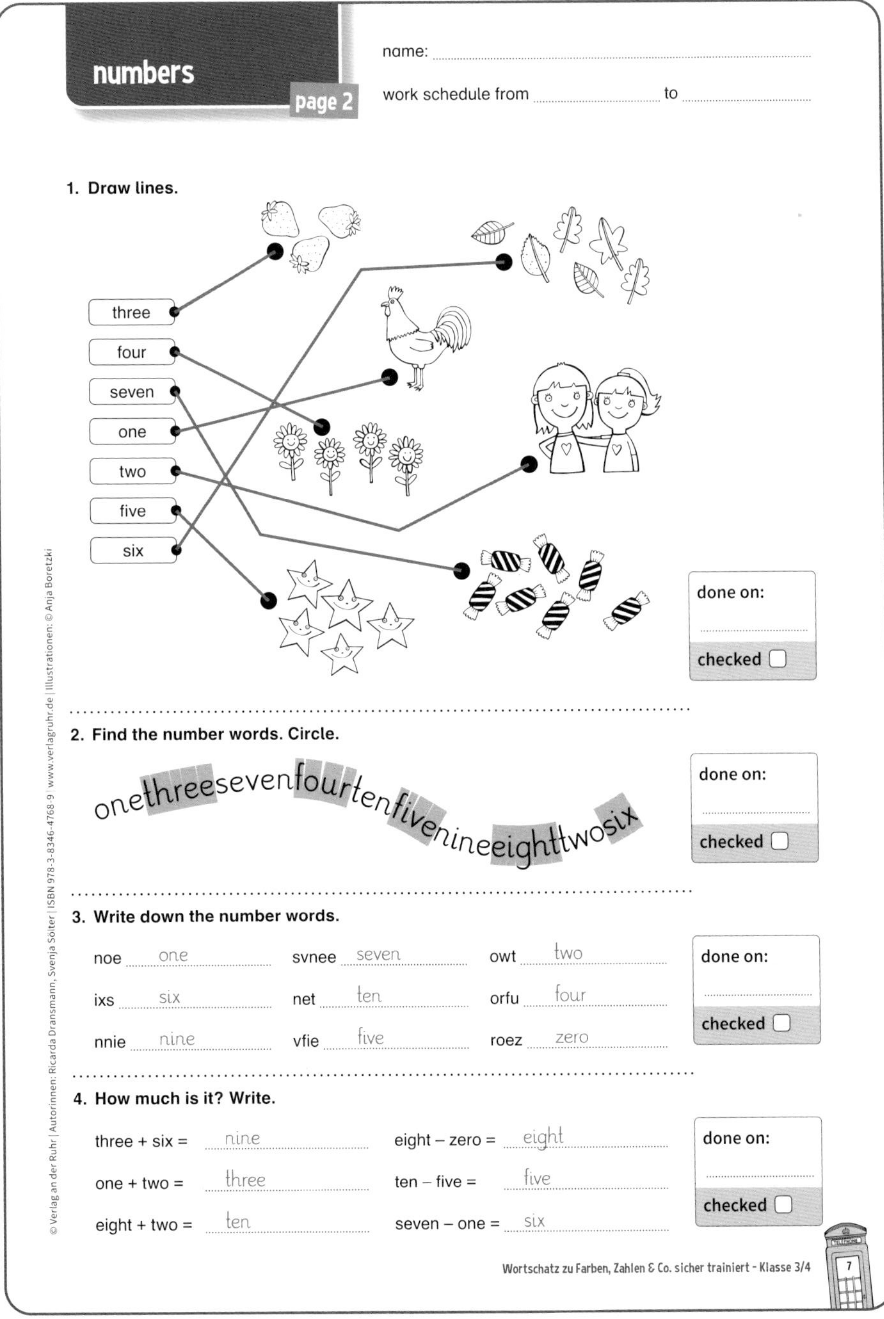
numbers page 2

name: ...

work schedule from ... to ...

1. Draw lines.

three · four · seven · one · two · five · six

done on: ... checked

2. Find the number words. Circle.

onethreesevenfourtenfivenineeighttwosix

done on: ... checked

3. Write down the number words.

noe one · svnee seven · owt two

ixs six · net ten · orfu four

nnie nine · vfie five · roez zero

done on: ... checked

4. How much is it? Write.

three + six = nine · eight – zero = eight

one + two = three · ten – five = five

eight + two = ten · seven – one = six

done on: ... checked



Wortschatz zu Farben, Zahlen & Co. sicher trainiert - Klasse 3/4 · 7

Lösungen

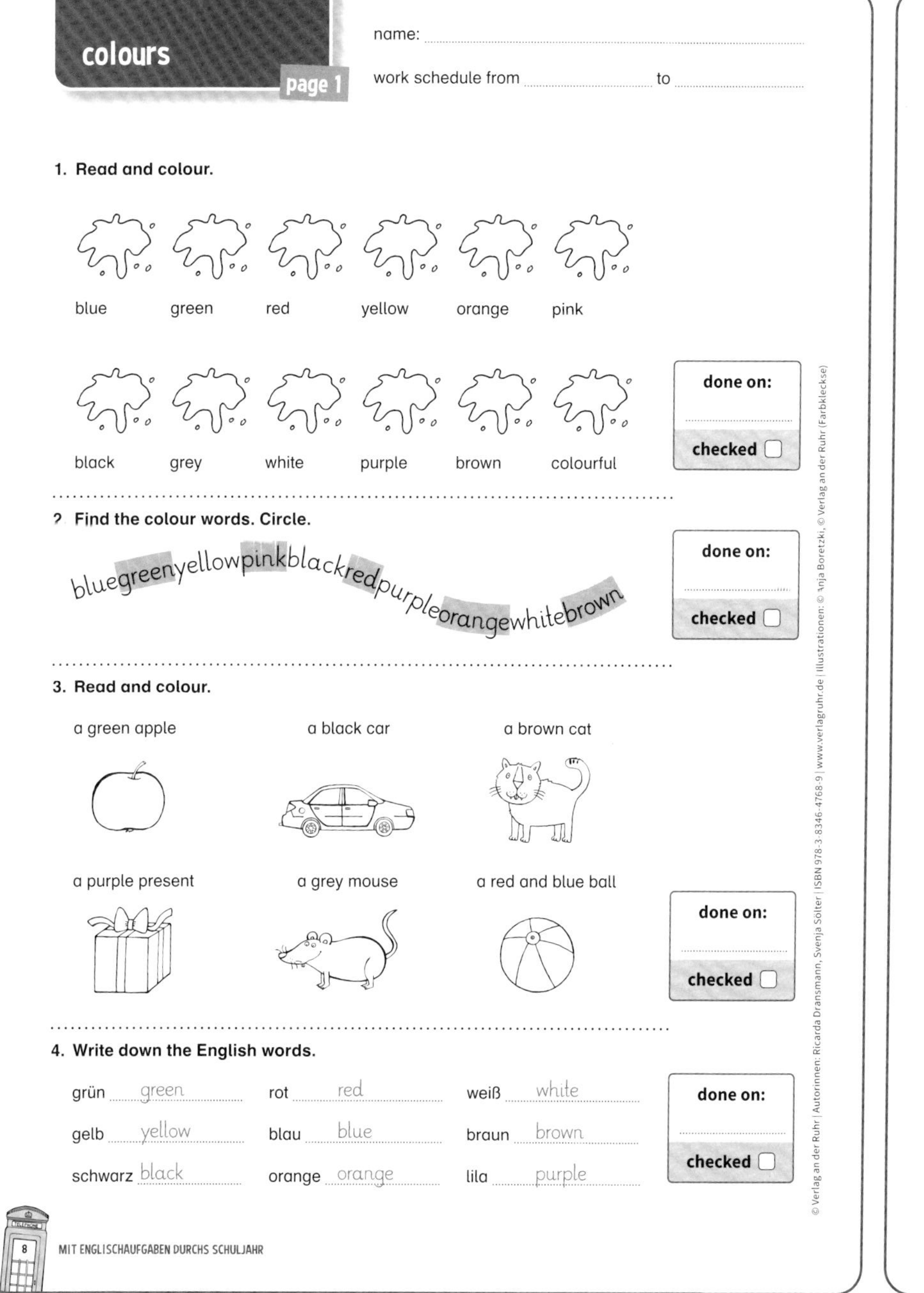

## colours
page 1

name: ..................

work schedule from .................. to ..................

**1. Read and colour.**

blue · green · red · yellow · orange · pink

black · grey · white · purple · brown · colourful

done on: ........ checked ☐

**2. Find the colour words. Circle.**

bluegreenyellowpinkblackredpurpleorangewhitebrown

done on: ........ checked ☐

**3. Read and colour.**

a green apple · a black car · a brown cat

a purple present · a grey mouse · a red and blue ball

done on: ........ checked ☐

**4. Write down the English words.**

grün green · rot red · weiß white

gelb yellow · blau blue · braun brown

schwarz black · orange orange · lila purple

done on: ........ checked ☐

8 MIT ENGLISCHAUFGABEN DURCHS SCHULJAHR



## colours
page 2

name: ..................

work schedule from .................. to ..................

**1. Find 10 colour words. Circle.**

| | | | | | | | |
|---|---|---|---|---|---|---|---|
| H | R | E | D | Y | A | G | P |
| B | D | G | I | P | L | R | I |
| L | W | B | L | U | E | E | N |
| A | H | S | K | R | I | Y | K |
| C | I | L | O | P | R | X | V |
| K | T | Y | E | L | L | O | W |
| J | E | G | R | E | E | N | M |
| M | S | B | R | O | W | N | F |

done on: ........ checked ☐

**2. Colour the T-shirts.**

blue + red · purple + pink · green + grey · yellow + brown

done on: ........ checked ☐

**3. Fill in the right letters.**

red · orange · blue · purple

yellow · colourful · white · brown

green · pink · grey · black

done on: ........ checked ☐

**4. Read and colour.**

Nick's hair is brown.
Nick's pullover is blue.
Jenny's hair is red.
Jenny's T-shirt is green.
Billy's hair is black.
Billy's T-shirt is pink and purple.

Nick · Jenny · Billy

done on: ........ checked ☐

Wortschatz zu Farben, Zahlen & Co. sicher trainiert - Klasse 3/4 9

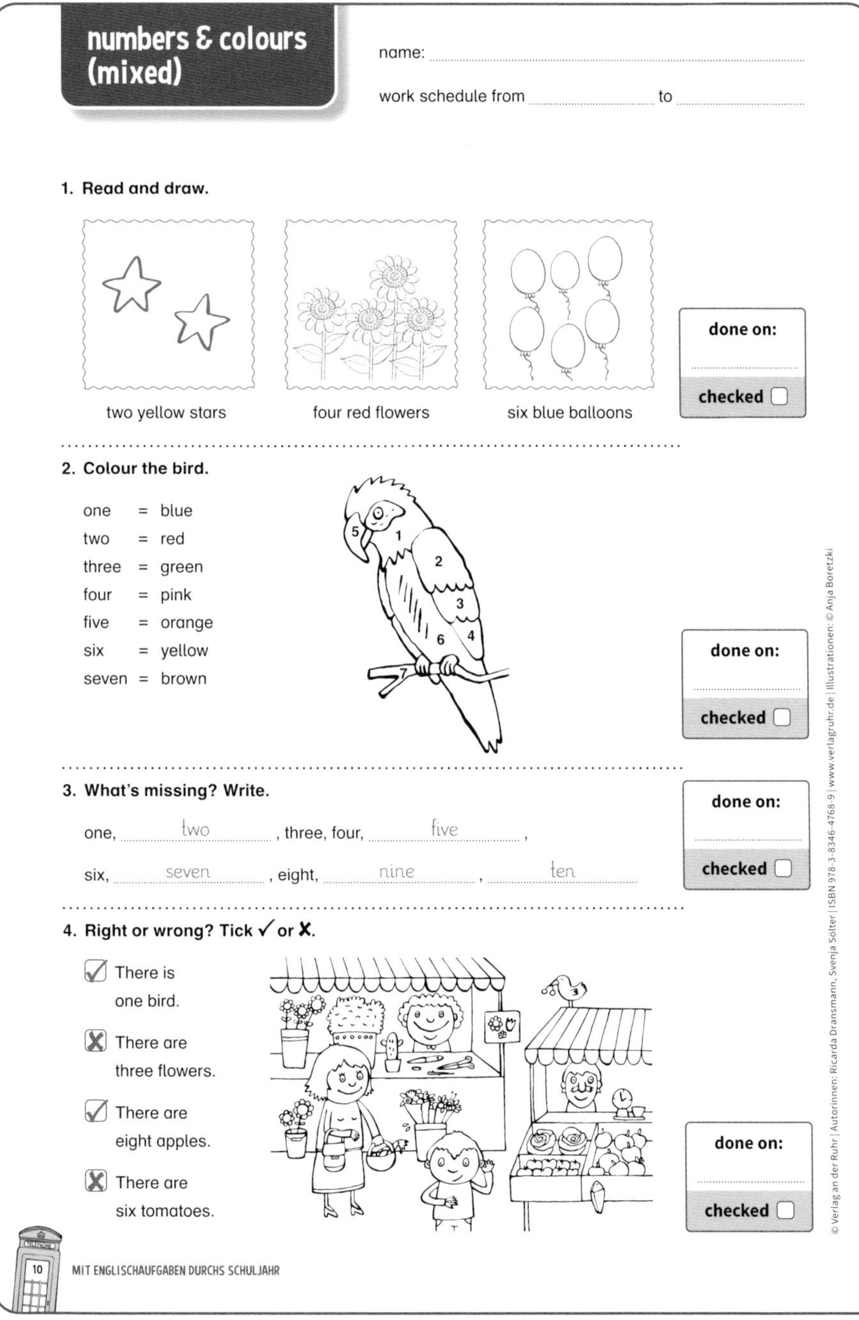

## numbers & colours (mixed)

name: ..................

work schedule from .................. to ..................

**1. Read and draw.**

two yellow stars — four red flowers — six blue balloons

done on: ..................
checked ☐

**2. Colour the bird.**

one = blue
two = red
three = green
four = pink
five = orange
six = yellow
seven = brown

done on: ..................
checked ☐

**3. What's missing? Write.**

one, two, three, four, five,
six, seven, eight, nine, ten

done on: ..................
checked ☐

**4. Right or wrong? Tick ✓ or ✗.**

☑ There is one bird.
☒ There are three flowers.
☑ There are eight apples.
☒ There are six tomatoes.

done on: ..................
checked ☐

10 MIT ENGLISCHAUFGABEN DURCHS SCHULJAHR



## my body

page 1

name: ..................

work schedule from .................. to ..................

**1. Fill in the right words.**

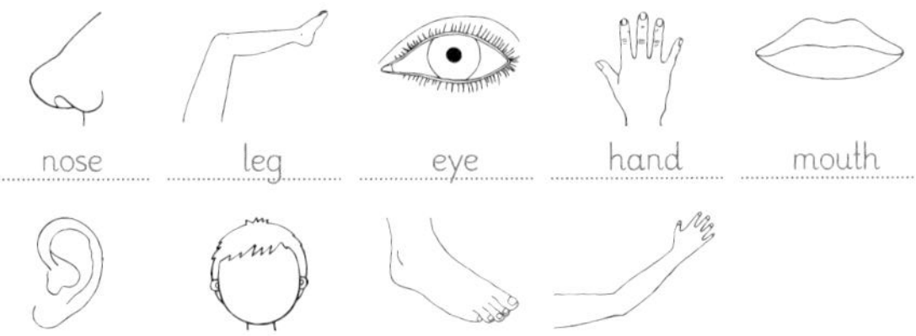

nose, leg, eye, hand, mouth

ear, head, foot, arm

~~eye~~ ~~hand~~ ~~head~~ ~~nose~~ ~~ear~~ ~~arm~~ ~~mouth~~ ~~leg~~ ~~foot~~

done on: ..................
checked ☐

**2. Find the body words. Circle.**

mouthhandeyeearnosefootheadlegarm

done on: ..................
checked ☐

**3. Do the crossword.**

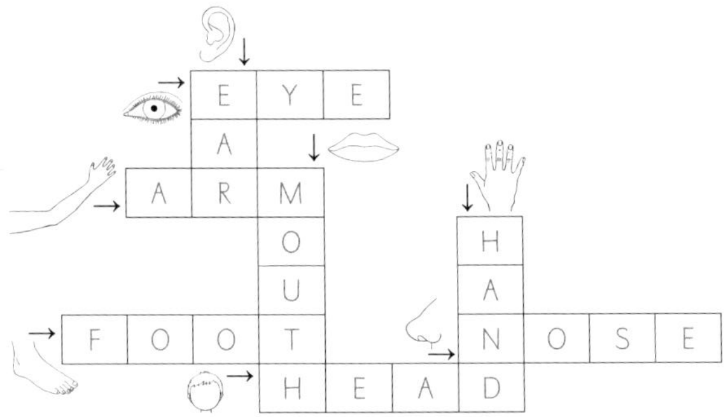

| | | | | | | | | | |
|---|---|---|---|---|---|---|---|---|---|
| | | E | Y | E | | | | | |
| | | A | | | | | | | |
| | A | R | M | | | | | | |
| | | | O | | | H | | | |
| | | | U | | | A | | | |
| F | O | O | T | | | N | O | S | E |
| | | | H | E | A | D | | | |

done on: ..................
checked ☐

**4. Complete the sentences.**

The monster has got three eyes.

The monster has got four legs.

The monster has got five arms.

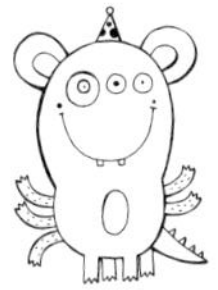

done on: ..................
checked ☐

Wortschatz zu Farben, Zahlen & Co. sicher trainiert – Klasse 3/4 11

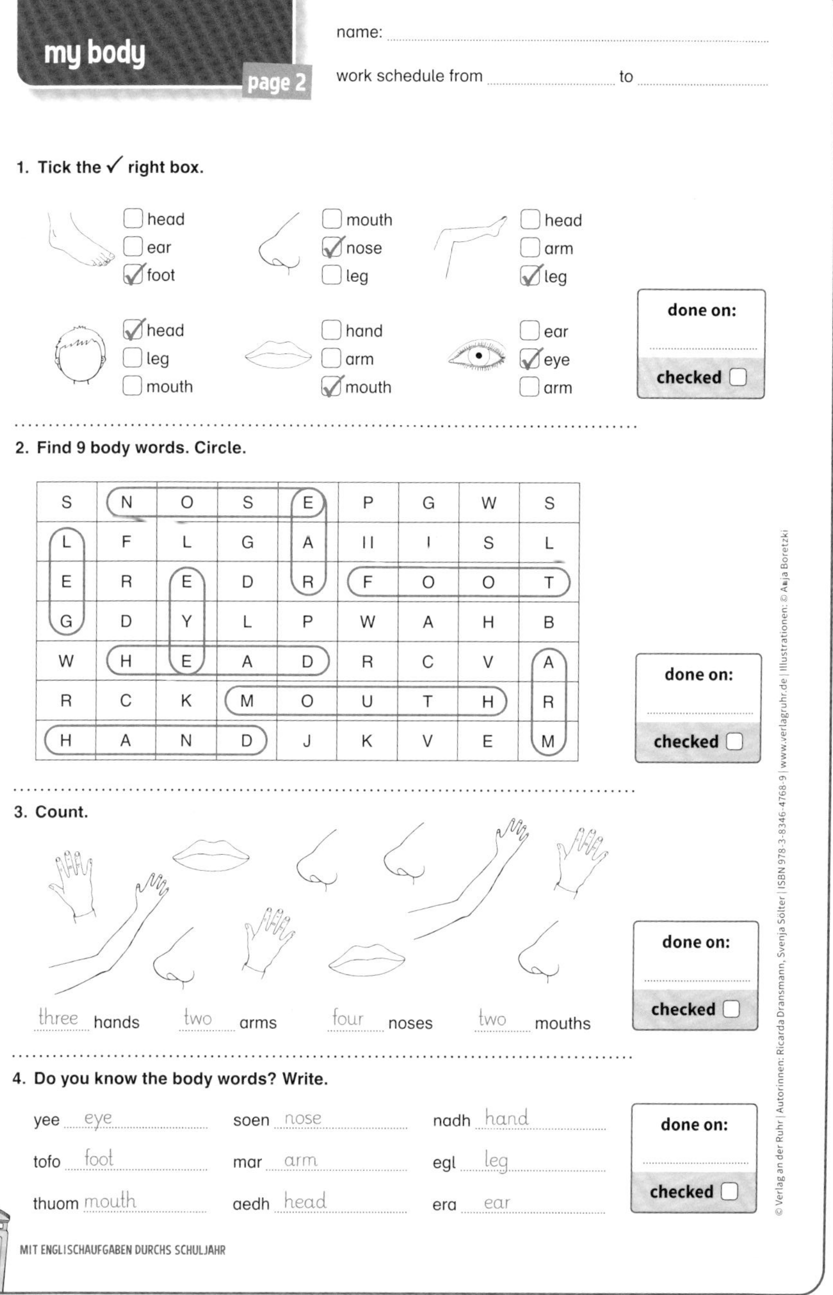

## my body

page 2

name: ............

work schedule from ............ to ............

1. Tick the ✓ right box.

☐ head ☐ ear ☑ foot

☐ mouth ☑ nose ☐ leg

☐ head ☐ arm ☑ leg

☑ head ☐ leg ☐ mouth

☐ hand ☐ arm ☑ mouth

☐ ear ☑ eye ☐ arm

done on: ............ checked ☐

2. Find 9 body words. Circle.

| S | N | O | S | E | P | G | W | S |
|---|---|---|---|---|---|---|---|---|
| L | F | L | G | A | I | I | S | L |
| E | R | E | D | R | F | O | O | T |
| G | D | Y | L | P | W | A | H | B |
| W | H | E | A | D | R | C | V | A |
| R | C | K | M | O | U | T | H | R |
| H | A | N | D | J | K | V | E | M |

done on: ............ checked ☐

3. Count.

three hands · two arms · four noses · two mouths

done on: ............ checked ☐

4. Do you know the body words? Write.

yee eye · soen nose · nadh hand

tofo foot · mar arm · egl leg

thuom mouth · aedh head · era ear

done on: ............ checked ☐

© Verlag an der Ruhr | Autorinnen: Ricarda Dransmann, Svenja Solter | ISBN 978-3-8346-4768-9 | www.verlagruhr.de | Illustrationen: © Anja Boretzki

12 MIT ENGLISCHAUFGABEN DURCHS SCHULJAHR

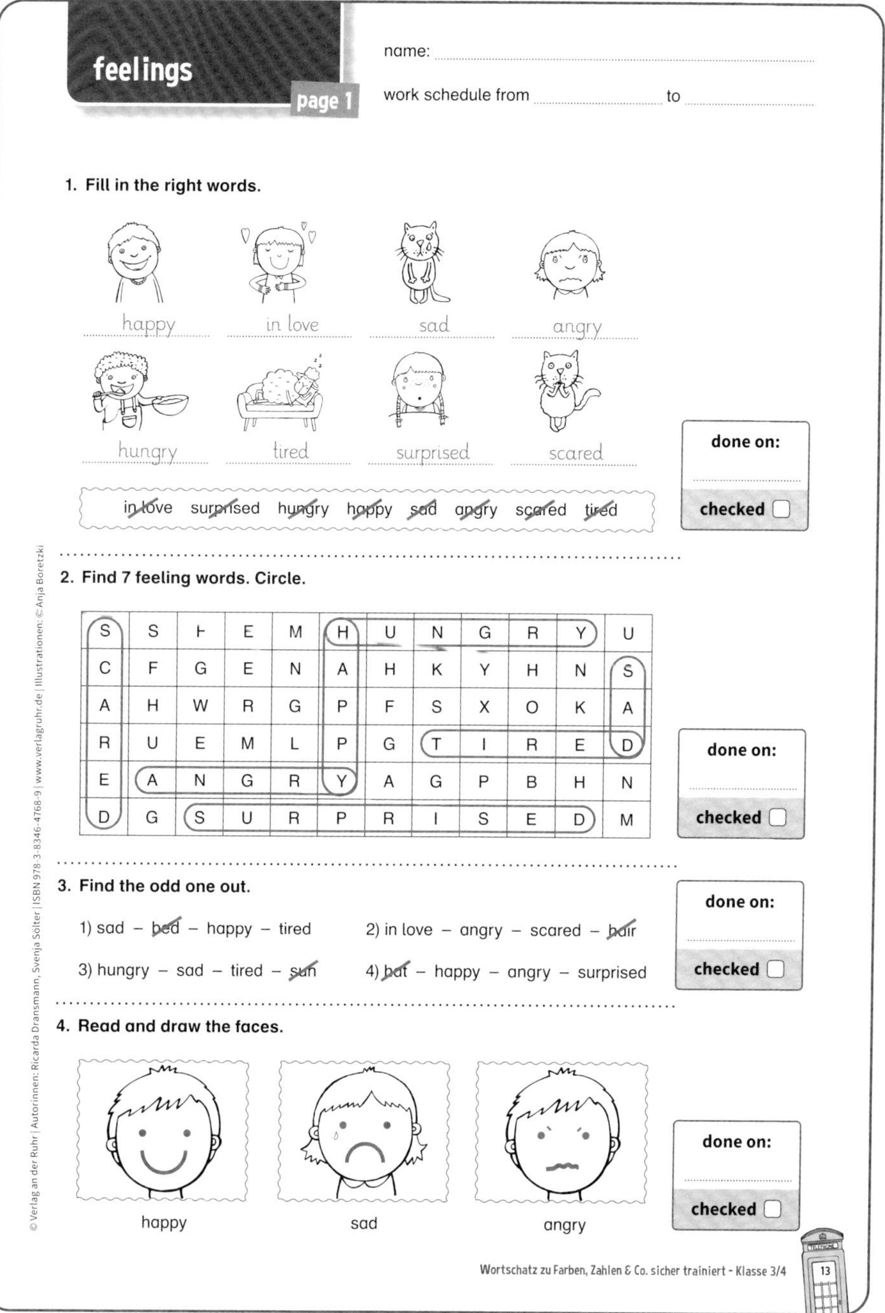

## feelings

page 1

name: ............

work schedule from ............ to ............

1. Fill in the right words.

happy · in love · sad · angry

hungry · tired · surprised · scared

~~in love~~ ~~surprised~~ ~~hungry~~ ~~happy~~ ~~sad~~ ~~angry~~ ~~scared~~ ~~tired~~

done on: ............ checked ☐

2. Find 7 feeling words. Circle.

| S | S | F | E | M | H | U | N | G | R | Y | U |
|---|---|---|---|---|---|---|---|---|---|---|---|
| C | F | G | E | N | A | H | K | Y | H | N | S |
| A | H | W | R | G | P | F | S | X | O | K | A |
| R | U | E | M | L | P | G | T | I | R | E | D |
| E | A | N | G | R | Y | A | G | P | B | H | N |
| D | G | S | U | R | P | R | I | S | E | D | M |

done on: ............ checked ☐

3. Find the odd one out.

1) sad – ~~bed~~ – happy – tired

2) in love – angry – scared – ~~hair~~

3) hungry – sad – tired – ~~sun~~

4) ~~bat~~ – happy – angry – surprised

done on: ............ checked ☐

4. Read and draw the faces.

happy · sad · angry

done on: ............ checked ☐

© Verlag an der Ruhr | Autorinnen: Ricarda Dransmann, Svenja Solter | ISBN 978-3-8346-4768-9 | www.verlagruhr.de | Illustrationen: © Anja Boretzki

Wortschatz zu Farben, Zahlen & Co. sicher trainiert - Klasse 3/4

13

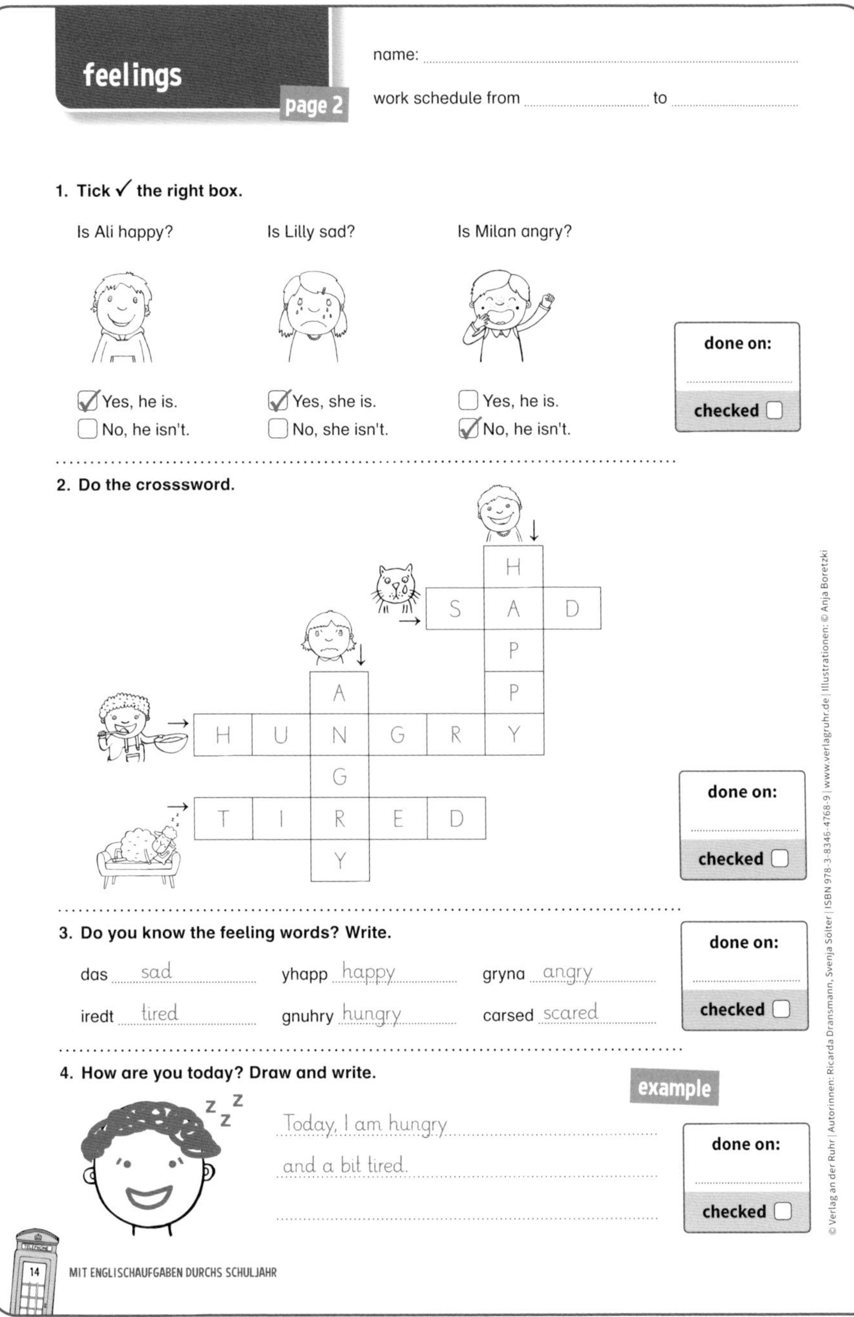

## feelings

page 2

name: ..................

work schedule from .......... to ..........

**1. Tick ✓ the right box.**

Is Ali happy? ☑ Yes, he is. ☐ No, he isn't.

Is Lilly sad? ☑ Yes, she is. ☐ No, she isn't.

Is Milan angry? ☐ Yes, he is. ☑ No, he isn't.

done on: ..........
checked ☐

**2. Do the crosssword.**



done on: ..........
checked ☐

**3. Do you know the feeling words? Write.**

das sad

yhapp happy

gryna angry

iredt tired

gnuhry hungry

carsed scared

done on: ..........
checked ☐

**4. How are you today? Draw and write.**

example

Today, I am hungry

and a bit tired.

done on: ..........
checked ☐





## fruit

page 1

name: ..................

work schedule from .......... to ..........

**1. Draw lines.**

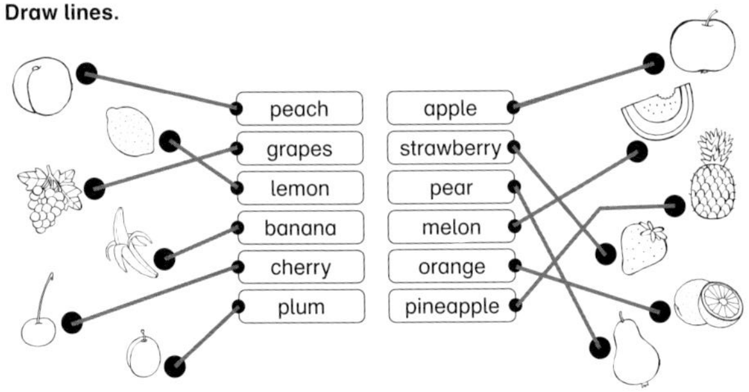

peach, grapes, lemon, banana, cherry, plum

apple, strawberry, pear, melon, orange, pineapple

done on: ..........
checked ☐

**2. Do you know the fruit words? Write.**

onlem melon

plepa apple

rryech cherry

yberrawstr strawberry

pppineale pineapple

achpe peach

done on: ..........
checked ☐

**3. Count.**

2 pears 4 strawberries 3 bananas 2 lemons

done on: ..........
checked ☐

**4. What's in your fruit salad? Draw and write.**

example

In my fruit salad, there are

a melon, strawberries

and cherries.

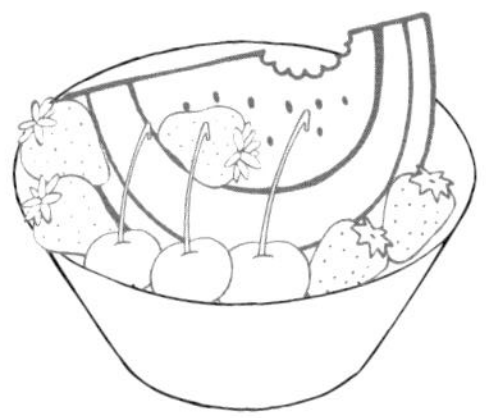

done on: ..........
checked ☐

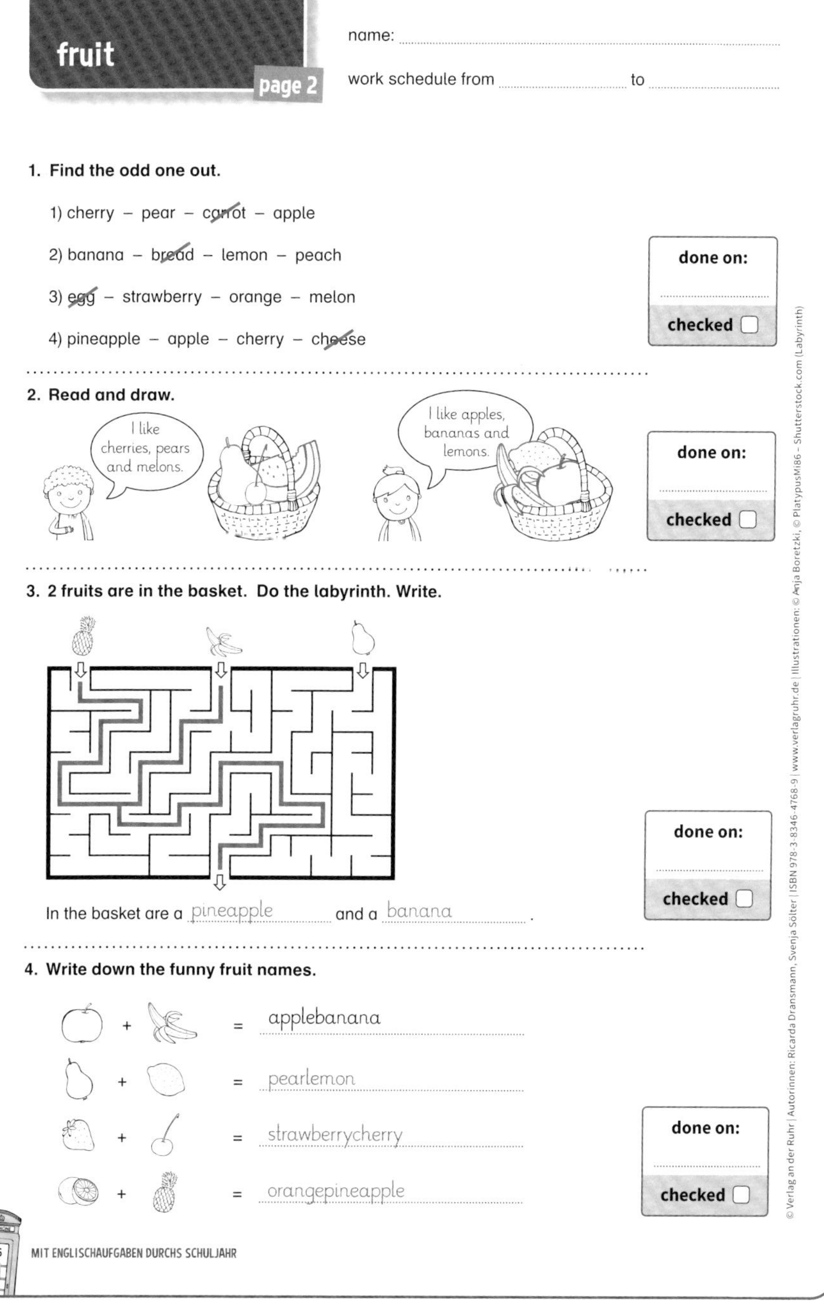

## fruit

page 2

name: ..................

work schedule from .................. to ..................

**1. Find the odd one out.**

1) cherry – pear – ~~carrot~~ – apple

2) banana – ~~bread~~ – lemon – peach

3) ~~egg~~ – strawberry – orange – melon

4) pineapple – apple – cherry – ~~cheese~~

done on: ..................
checked ☐

**2. Read and draw.**



done on: ..................
checked ☐

**3. 2 fruits are in the basket. Do the labyrinth. Write.**

In the basket are a pineapple and a banana.

done on: ..................
checked ☐

**4. Write down the funny fruit names.**

= applebanana

= pearlemon

= strawberrycherry

= orangepineapple

done on: ..................
checked ☐

MIT ENGLISCHAUFGABEN DURCHS SCHULJAHR 16

© Verlag an der Ruhr | Autorinnen: Ricarda Dransmann, Svenja Sölter | ISBN 978-3-8346-4768-9 | www.verlagruhr.de | Illustrationen: © Anja Boretzki, © PlatypusMi86 - Shutterstock.com (Labyrinth)

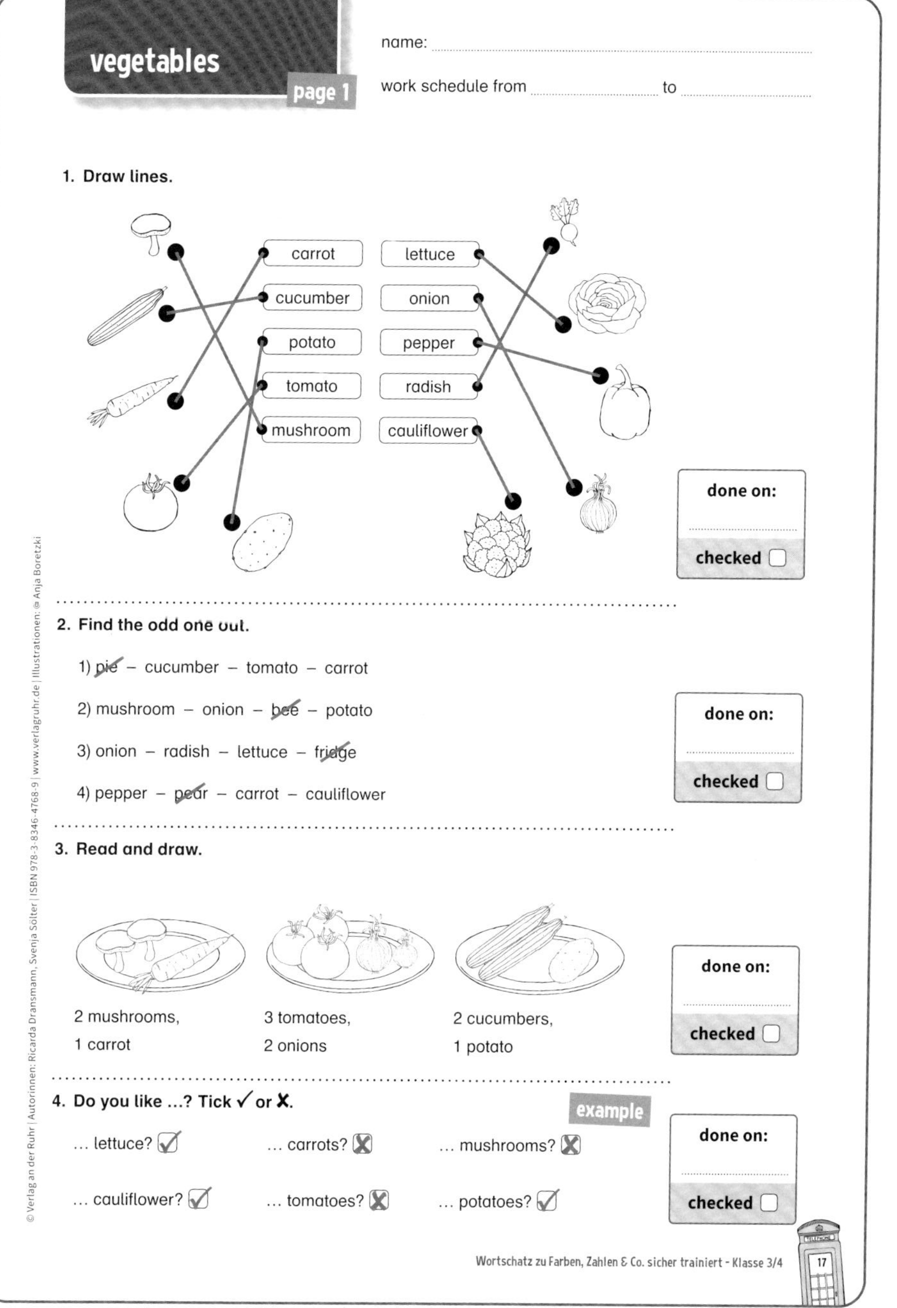

## vegetables

page 1

name: ..................

work schedule from .................. to ..................

**1. Draw lines.**

carrot – cucumber – potato – tomato – mushroom

lettuce – onion – pepper – radish – cauliflower

done on: ..................
checked ☐

**2. Find the odd one out.**

1) ~~pie~~ – cucumber – tomato – carrot

2) mushroom – onion – ~~bee~~ – potato

3) onion – radish – lettuce – ~~fridge~~

4) pepper – ~~pear~~ – carrot – cauliflower

done on: ..................
checked ☐

**3. Read and draw.**

2 mushrooms, 1 carrot

3 tomatoes, 2 onions

2 cucumbers, 1 potato

done on: ..................
checked ☐

**4. Do you like ...? Tick ✓ or ✗.**

example: ... mushrooms? ✗ ... potatoes? ✓

... lettuce? ✓ ... carrots? ✗

... cauliflower? ✓ ... tomatoes? ✗

done on: ..................
checked ☐

© Verlag an der Ruhr | Autorinnen: Ricarda Dransmann, Svenja Sölter | ISBN 978-3-8346-4768-9 | www.verlagruhr.de | Illustrationen: © Anja Boretzki

Wortschatz zu Farben, Zahlen & Co. sicher trainiert - Klasse 3/4 17

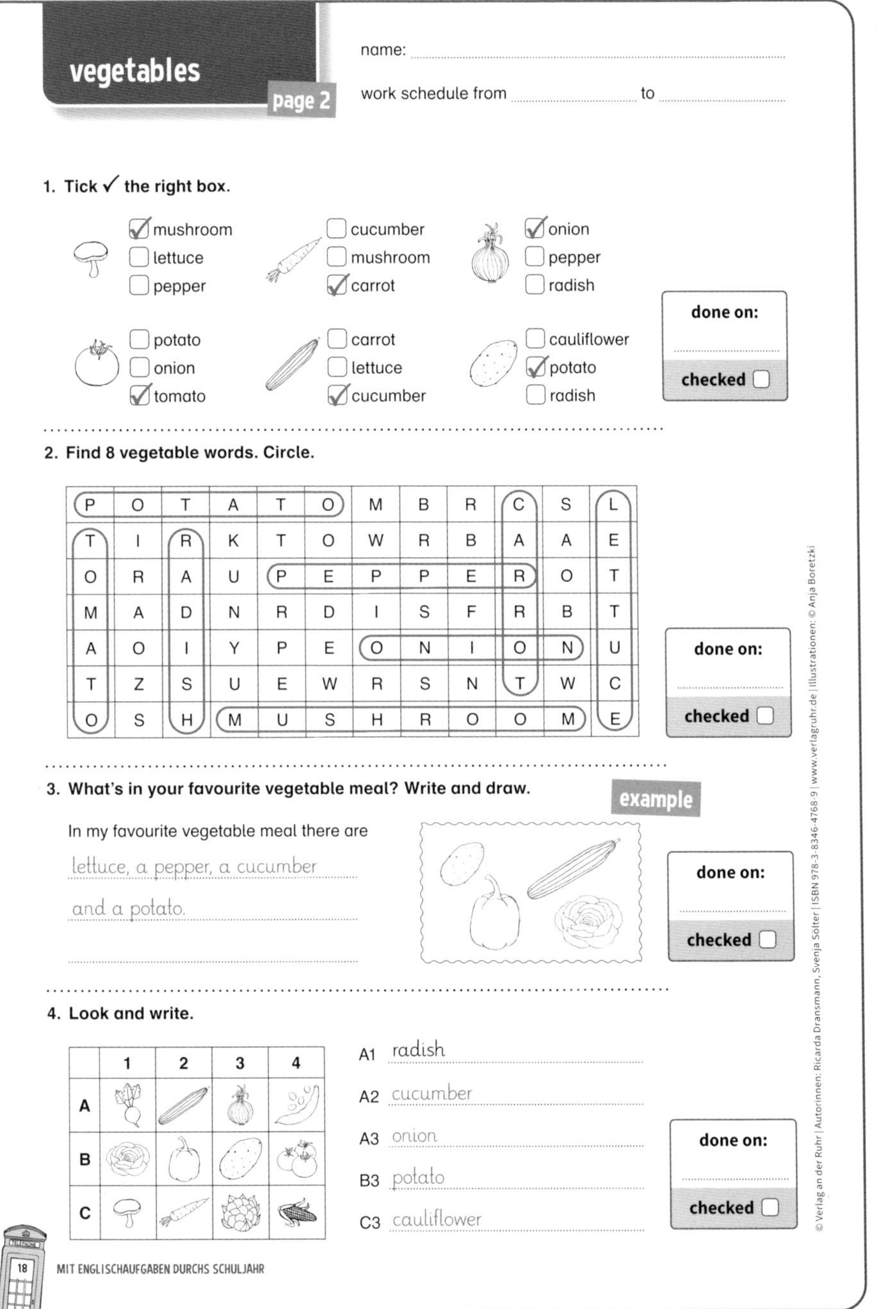

## vegetables
page 2

name: ......

work schedule from ...... to ......

**1. Tick ✓ the right box.**

- [x] mushroom
- [ ] lettuce
- [ ] pepper

- [ ] cucumber
- [ ] mushroom
- [x] carrot

- [x] onion
- [ ] pepper
- [ ] radish

- [ ] potato
- [ ] onion
- [x] tomato

- [ ] carrot
- [ ] lettuce
- [x] cucumber

- [ ] cauliflower
- [x] potato
- [ ] radish

done on: ...... checked ☐

**2. Find 8 vegetable words. Circle.**

| | | | | | | | | | | | |
|---|---|---|---|---|---|---|---|---|---|---|---|
| P | O | T | A | T | O | M | B | R | C | S | L |
| T | I | R | K | T | O | W | R | B | A | A | E |
| O | R | A | U | P | E | P | P | E | R | O | T |
| M | A | D | N | R | D | I | S | F | R | B | T |
| A | O | I | Y | P | E | O | N | I | O | N | U |
| T | Z | S | U | E | W | R | S | N | T | W | C |
| O | S | H | M | U | S | H | R | O | O | M | E |

done on: ...... checked ☐

**3. What's in your favourite vegetable meal? Write and draw.**

example

In my favourite vegetable meal there are lettuce, a pepper, a cucumber and a potato.

done on: ...... checked ☐

**4. Look and write.**

| | 1 | 2 | 3 | 4 |
|---|---|---|---|---|
| A | | | | |
| B | | | | |
| C | | | | |

A1 radish
A2 cucumber
A3 onion
B3 potato
C3 cauliflower

done on: ...... checked ☐



© Verlag an der Ruhr | Autorinnen: Ricarda Dransmann, Svenja Solter | ISBN 978-3-8346-4768-9 | www.verlagruhr.de | Illustrationen: © Anja Boretzki

## fruit & vegetables (mixed)

name: ......

work schedule from ...... to ......

**1. Write down the fruit and vegetable words.**

fruit:
pear, strawberry, grapes,
orange

vegetable:
onion, tomato, carrot,
radish

done on: ...... checked ☐

**2. Find the fruit and vegetable words. Circle.**

lettuceorangeradishonionmelontomatoapplepepperpeachpotato

done on: ...... checked ☐

**3. Write the names on the boxes.**

cucumbers, strawberries, bananas
carrots, pears, tomatoes

done on: ...... checked ☐

**4. Write down the English shopping list.**

Melone
Paprika
Radieschen
Salat

melon
pepper
radish
lettuce

done on: ...... checked ☐

© Verlag an der Ruhr | Autorinnen: Ricarda Dransmann, Svenja Solter | ISBN 978-3-8346-4768-9 | www.verlagruhr.de | Illustrationen: © Anja Boretzki

# Lösungen

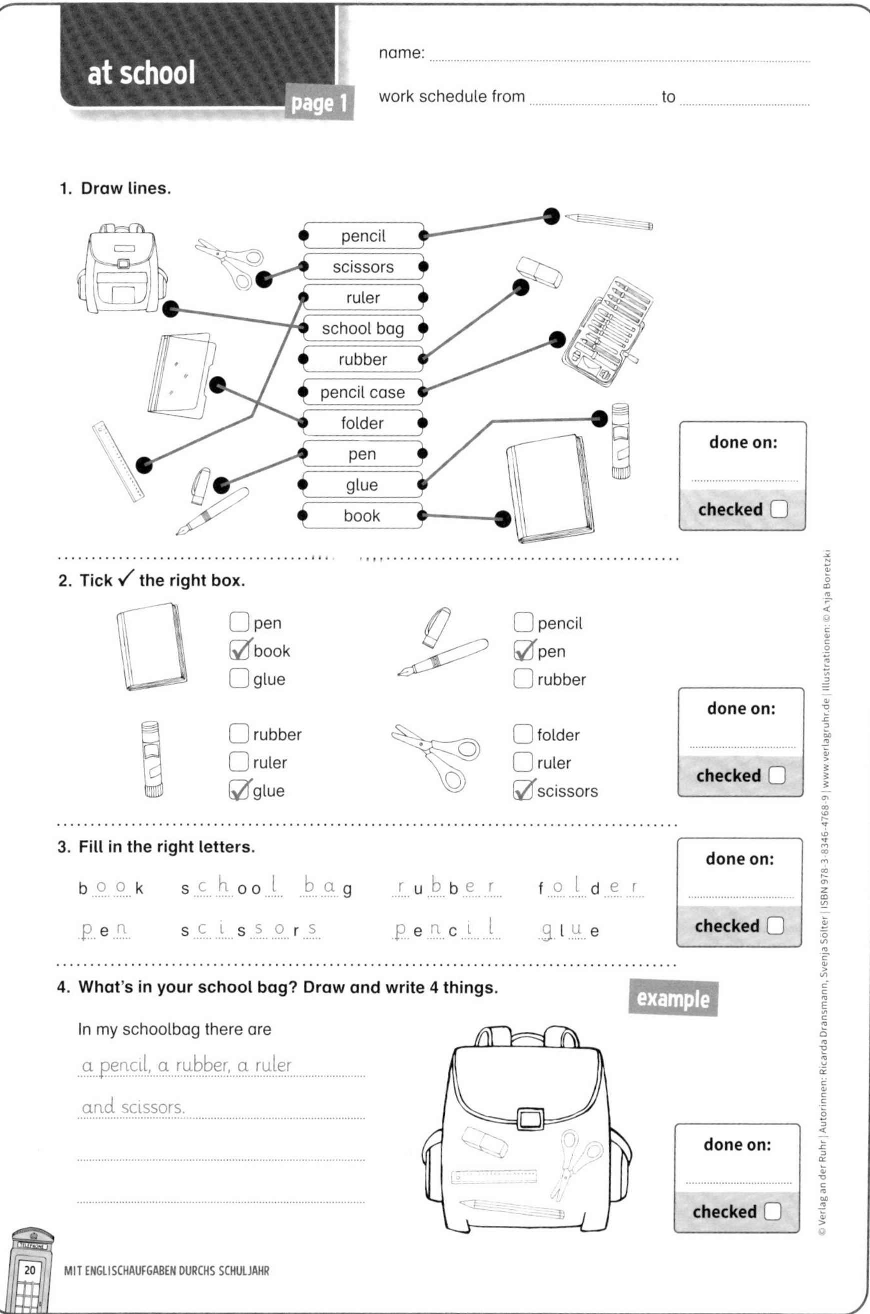

## at school – page 1

name: ..................

work schedule from .................. to ..................

1. Draw lines.

pencil, scissors, ruler, school bag, rubber, pencil case, folder, pen, glue, book

done on: ..... checked ☐

2. Tick ✓ the right box.

- ☐ pen ☑ book ☐ glue
- ☐ pencil ☑ pen ☐ rubber
- ☐ rubber ☐ ruler ☑ glue
- ☐ folder ☐ ruler ☑ scissors

done on: ..... checked ☐

3. Fill in the right letters.

book school bag rubber folder

pen scissors pencil glue

done on: ..... checked ☐

4. What's in your school bag? Draw and write 4 things.

example

In my schoolbag there are

a pencil, a rubber, a ruler

and scissors.

done on: ..... checked ☐

20 MIT ENGLISCHAUFGABEN DURCHS SCHULJAHR



## at school – page 2

name: ..................

work schedule from .................. to ..................

1. Find the school words. Circle.

scissorsrulerbookgluepencilrubberfolderpen

done on: ..... checked ☐

2. Look and write.

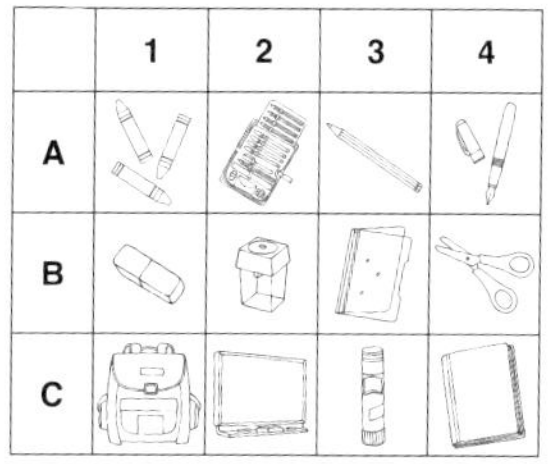

| | 1 | 2 | 3 | 4 |
|---|---|---|---|---|
| A | | | | |
| B | | | | |
| C | | | | |

A3 pencil

A4 pen

B1 rubber

B3 folder

C1 school bag

C4 book

done on: ..... checked ☐

3. Do the crossword.

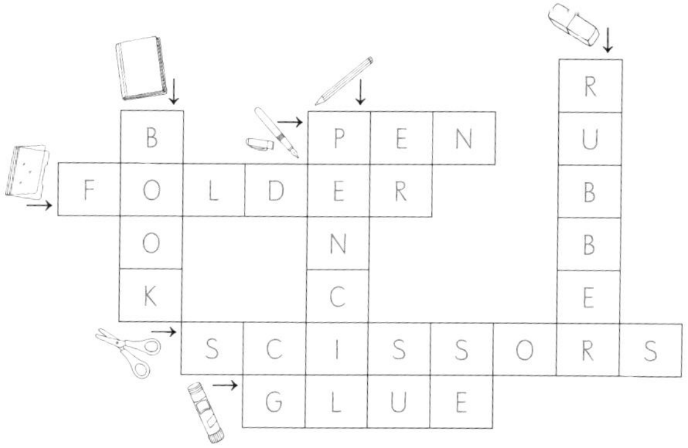

Across: PEN, FOLDER, SCISSORS, GLUE

Down: BOOK, PENCIL, RUBBER

done on: ..... checked ☐

4. What's on the desk? Write.

On the desk there are

a rubber, a book,

scissors and a pencil.

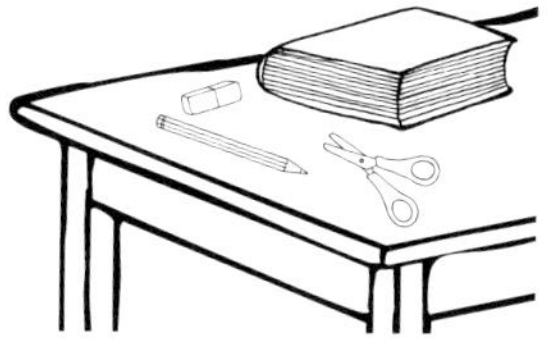

done on: ..... checked ☐

Wortschatz zu Farben, Zahlen & Co. sicher trainiert - Klasse 3/4 21

# Lösungen

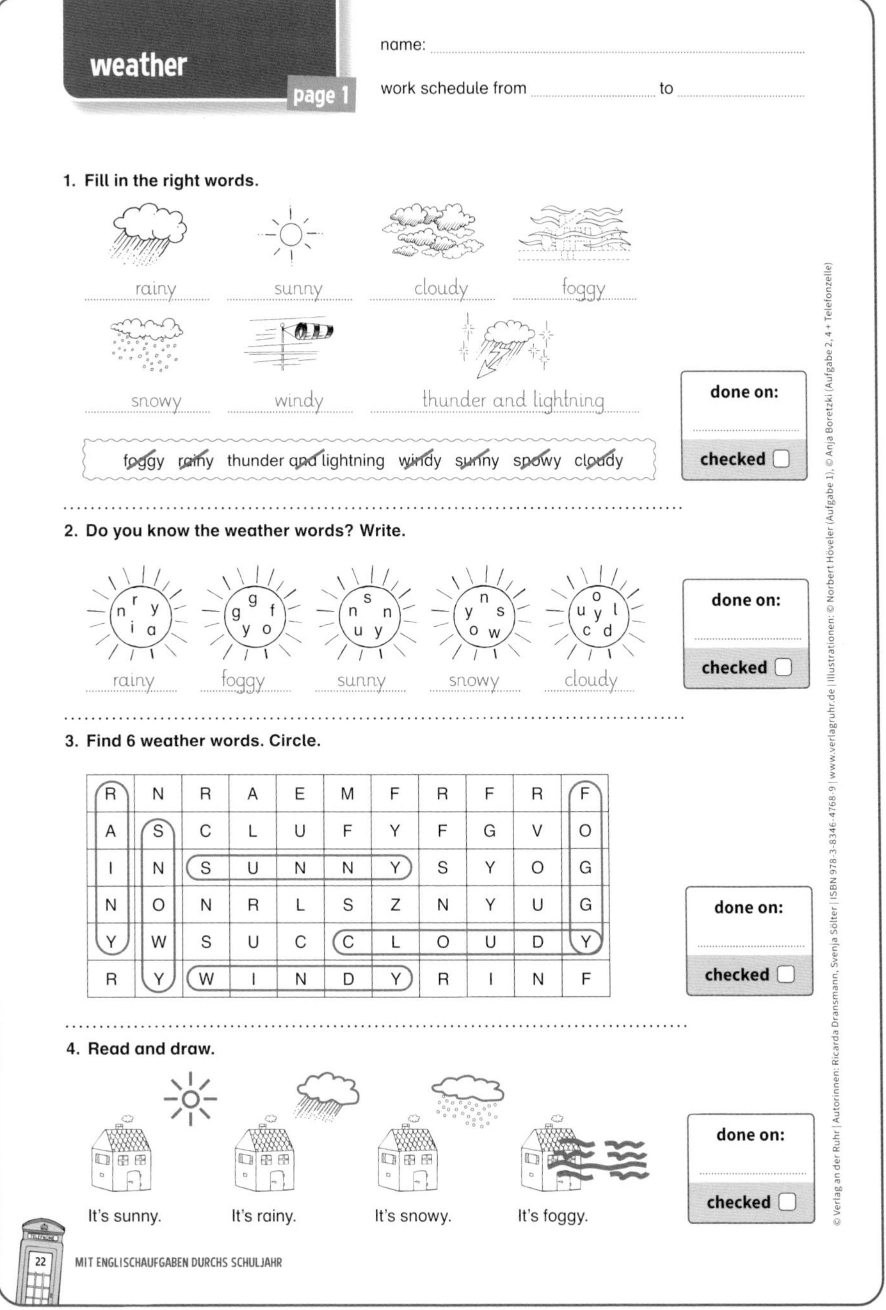

## weather – page 1

name: ...............

work schedule from ............... to ...............

**1. Fill in the right words.**

rainy · sunny · cloudy · foggy

snowy · windy · thunder and lightning

~~foggy~~ ~~rainy~~ thunder ~~and~~ lightning ~~windy~~ ~~sunny~~ ~~snowy~~ ~~cloudy~~

**done on:** ............... **checked** ☐

**2. Do you know the weather words? Write.**

n r y i a – rainy

g f y o g – foggy

s n n u y – sunny

n y s o w – snowy

o u y l c d – cloudy

**done on:** ............... **checked** ☐

**3. Find 6 weather words. Circle.**

| | | | | | | | | | | |
|---|---|---|---|---|---|---|---|---|---|---|
| R | N | R | A | E | M | F | R | F | R | F |
| A | S | C | L | U | F | Y | F | G | V | O |
| I | N | S | U | N | N | Y | S | Y | O | G |
| N | O | N | R | L | S | Z | N | Y | U | G |
| Y | W | S | U | C | C | L | O | U | D | Y |
| R | Y | W | I | N | D | Y | R | I | N | F |

**done on:** ............... **checked** ☐

**4. Read and draw.**

It's sunny. It's rainy. It's snowy. It's foggy.

**done on:** ............... **checked** ☐





## weather – page 2

name: ...............

work schedule from ............... to ...............

**1. Fill in the right numbers.**

(1) sunny
(2) cloudy
(3) windy
(4) rainy
(5) foggy
(6) thunder and lightning
(7) snowy

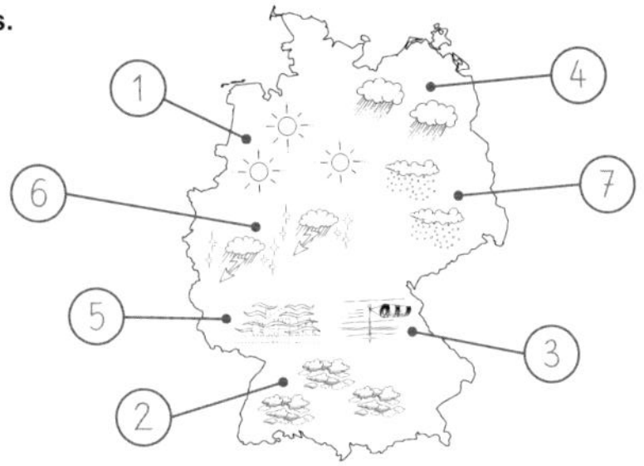

**done on:** ............... **checked** ☐

**2. Find the odd one out.**

1) windy – sunny – ~~happy~~ – snowy

2) sunny – foggy – rainy – ~~thirsty~~

3) ~~funny~~ – windy – snowy – cloudy

4) cloudy – rainy – sunny – ~~silly~~

**done on:** ............... **checked** ☐

**3. Fill in the right words.**

We go to the beach. It's sunny.

I can't see very much. It's foggy.

We build a snowman. It's snowy.

I need my umbrella. It's rainy.

We fly a kite. It's windy.

~~snowy~~ ~~windy~~ ~~sunny~~ ~~rainy~~ ~~foggy~~

**done on:** ............... **checked** ☐

**4. What's the weather like today? Draw and write.**

example

Today, it's

sunny and cloudy.

**done on:** ............... **checked** ☐

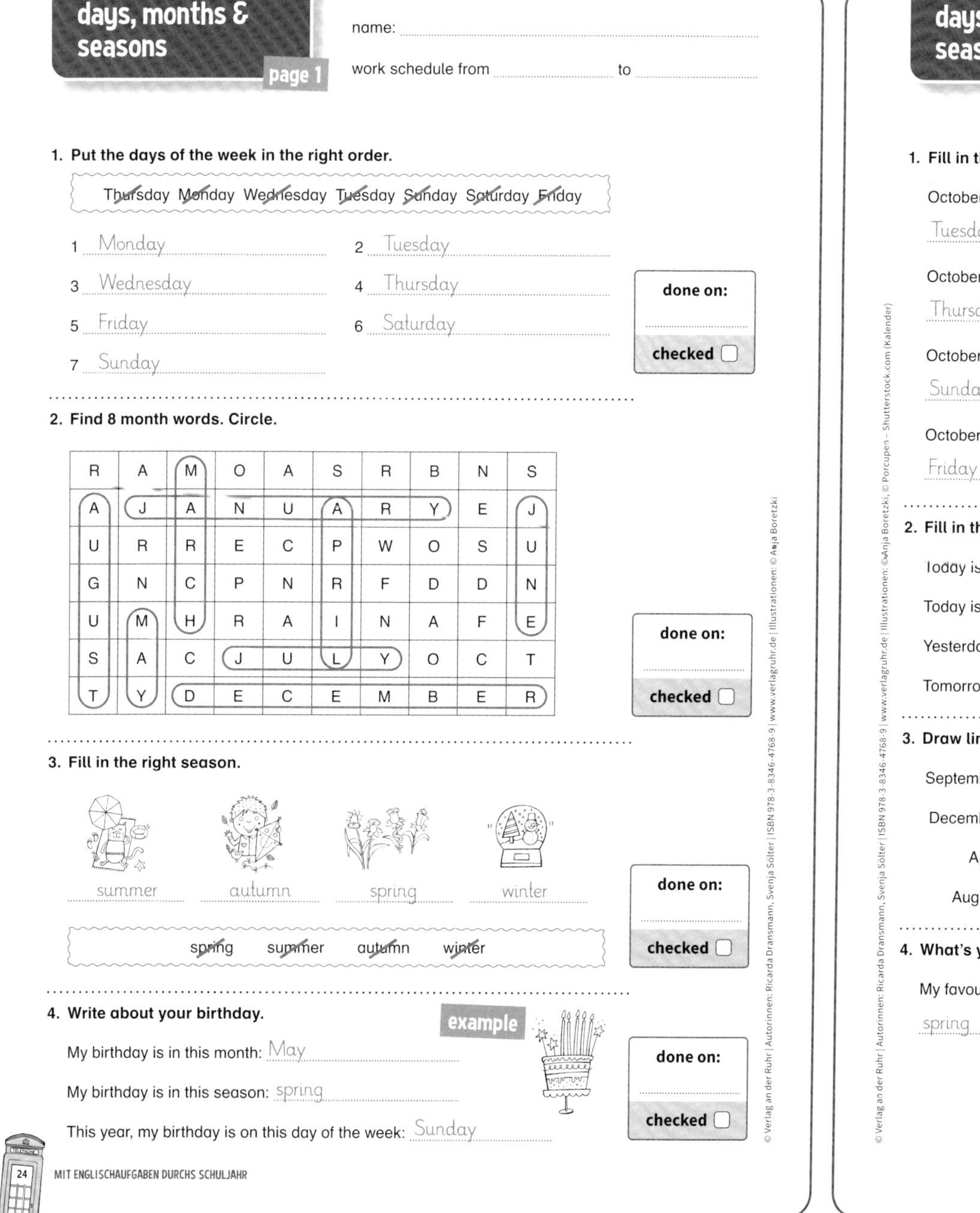

## days, months & seasons

page 1

name: ..........

work schedule from .......... to ..........

**1. Put the days of the week in the right order.**

Thursday Monday Wednesday Tuesday Sunday Saturday Friday

1 Monday 2 Tuesday
3 Wednesday 4 Thursday
5 Friday 6 Saturday
7 Sunday

done on: ..........
checked ☐

**2. Find 8 month words. Circle.**

| | | | | | | | | | |
|---|---|---|---|---|---|---|---|---|---|
| R | A | M | O | A | S | R | B | N | S |
| A | J | A | N | U | A | R | Y | E | J |
| U | R | R | E | C | P | W | O | S | U |
| G | N | C | P | N | R | F | D | D | N |
| U | M | H | R | A | I | N | A | F | E |
| S | A | C | J | U | L | Y | O | C | T |
| T | Y | D | E | C | E | M | B | E | R |

done on: ..........
checked ☐

**3. Fill in the right season.**

summer autumn spring winter

spring summer autumn winter

done on: ..........
checked ☐

**4. Write about your birthday.**

example

My birthday is in this month: May

My birthday is in this season: spring

This year, my birthday is on this day of the week: Sunday

done on: ..........
checked ☐





## days, months & seasons

page 2

name: ..........

work schedule from .......... to ..........

**1. Fill in the right day of the week.**

October 5:
Tuesday

October 14:
Thursday

October 24:
Sunday

October 29:
Friday

OCTOBER 2021

| MON | TUE | WED | THU | FRI | SAT | SUN |
|---|---|---|---|---|---|---|
| | | | | 1 | 2 | 3 |
| 4 | 5 | 6 | 7 | 8 | 9 | 10 |
| 11 | 12 | 13 | 14 | 15 | 16 | 17 |
| 18 | 19 | 20 | 21 | 22 | 23 | 24 |
| 25 | 26 | 27 | 28 | 29 | 30 | 31 |

done on: ..........
checked ☐

**2. Fill in the right day of the week.**

Today is Monday. Tomorrow is Tuesday.

Today is Sunday. Yesterday was Saturday.

Yesterday was Friday. Today is Saturday.

Tomorrow is Thursday. Today is Wednesday.

done on: ..........
checked ☐

**3. Draw lines.**

September, December, April, August

spring, summer, autumn, winter

July, February, October, March

done on: ..........
checked ☐

**4. What's your favourite season? Write and draw.**

example

My favourite season is

spring

done on: ..........
checked ☐

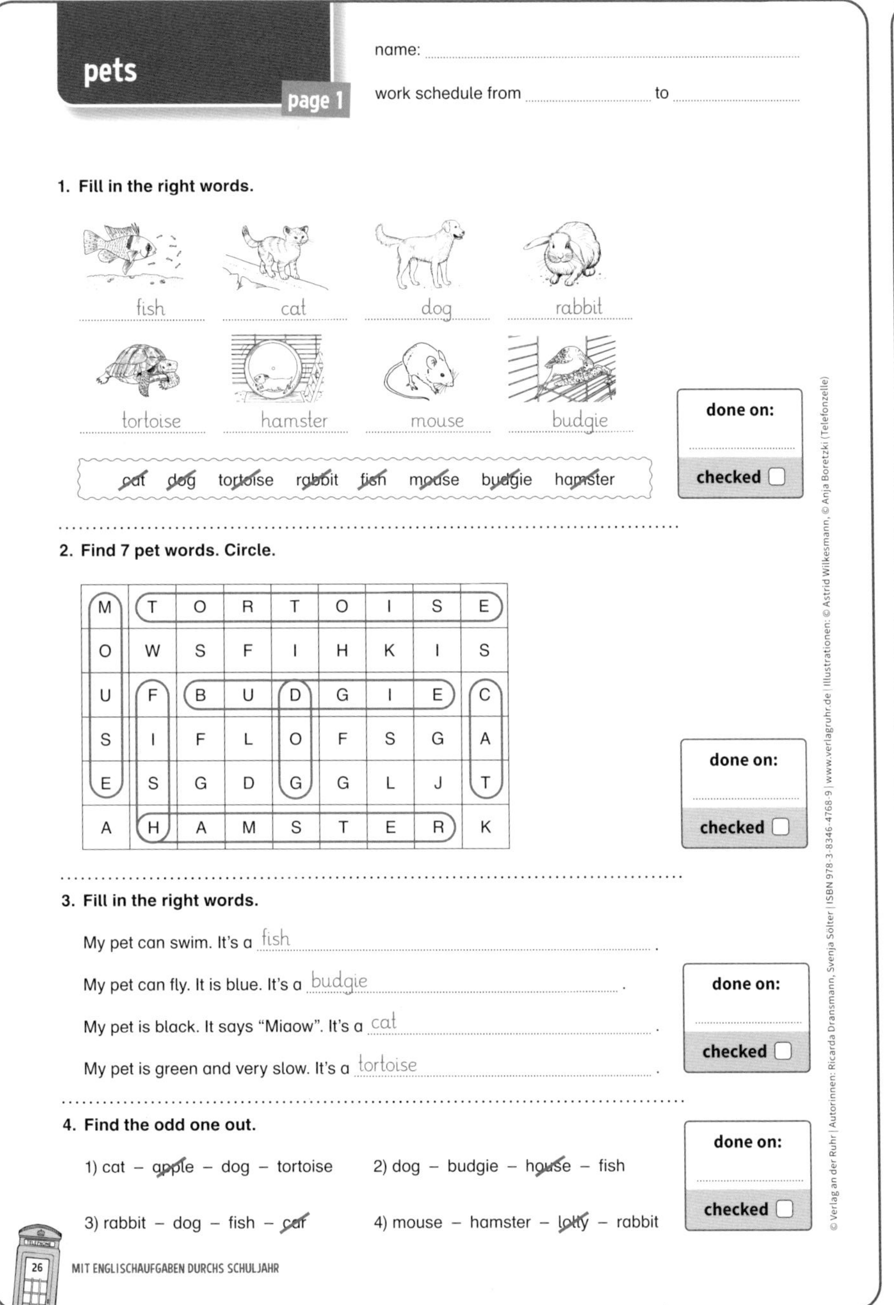

## pets

page 1

name: ..........

work schedule from .......... to ..........

**1. Fill in the right words.**

fish · cat · dog · rabbit

tortoise · hamster · mouse · budgie

~~cat~~ ~~dog~~ ~~tortoise~~ ~~rabbit~~ ~~fish~~ ~~mouse~~ ~~budgie~~ ~~hamster~~

done on: checked ☐

**2. Find 7 pet words. Circle.**

| | | | | | | | | |
|---|---|---|---|---|---|---|---|---|
| M | T | O | R | T | O | I | S | E |
| O | W | S | F | I | H | K | I | S |
| U | F | B | U | D | G | I | E | C |
| S | I | F | L | O | F | S | G | A |
| E | S | G | D | G | G | L | J | T |
| A | H | A | M | S | T | E | R | K |

done on: checked ☐

**3. Fill in the right words.**

My pet can swim. It's a fish.

My pet can fly. It is blue. It's a budgie.

My pet is black. It says "Miaow". It's a cat.

My pet is green and very slow. It's a tortoise.

done on: checked ☐

**4. Find the odd one out.**

1) cat – ~~apple~~ – dog – tortoise

2) dog – budgie – ~~house~~ – fish

3) rabbit – dog – fish – ~~car~~

4) mouse – hamster – ~~lolly~~ – rabbit

done on: checked ☐

26 MIT ENGLISCHAUFGABEN DURCHS SCHULJAHR



## pets

page 2

name: ..........

work schedule from .......... to ..........

**1. Tick ✓ the right box.**

☑ dog ☐ rabbit ☐ mouse

☐ cat ☑ rabbit ☐ hamster

☑ tortoise ☐ fish ☐ hamster

☑ budgie ☐ cat ☐ tortoise

done on: checked ☐

**2. Fill in the right letters.**

d o g · h a m s t e r · r a b b i t

m o u s e · b u d g i e · t o r t o i s e

done on: checked ☐

**3. Whose is it? Write.**

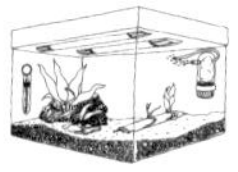

fish · dog · rabbit

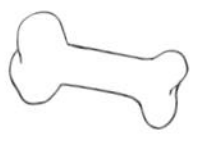

budgie · hamster · cat

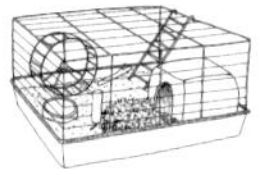

~~budgie~~ ~~hamster~~ ~~dog~~ ~~fish~~ ~~rabbit~~ ~~cat~~

done on: checked ☐

**4. What's your favourite pet? Write and draw.**

example

My favourite pet is a

dog.

It is brown (colour).

It likes meat and carrots

.......... (food).

done on: checked ☐



Wortschatz zu Farben, Zahlen & Co. sicher trainiert - Klasse 3/4 27

# Lösungen

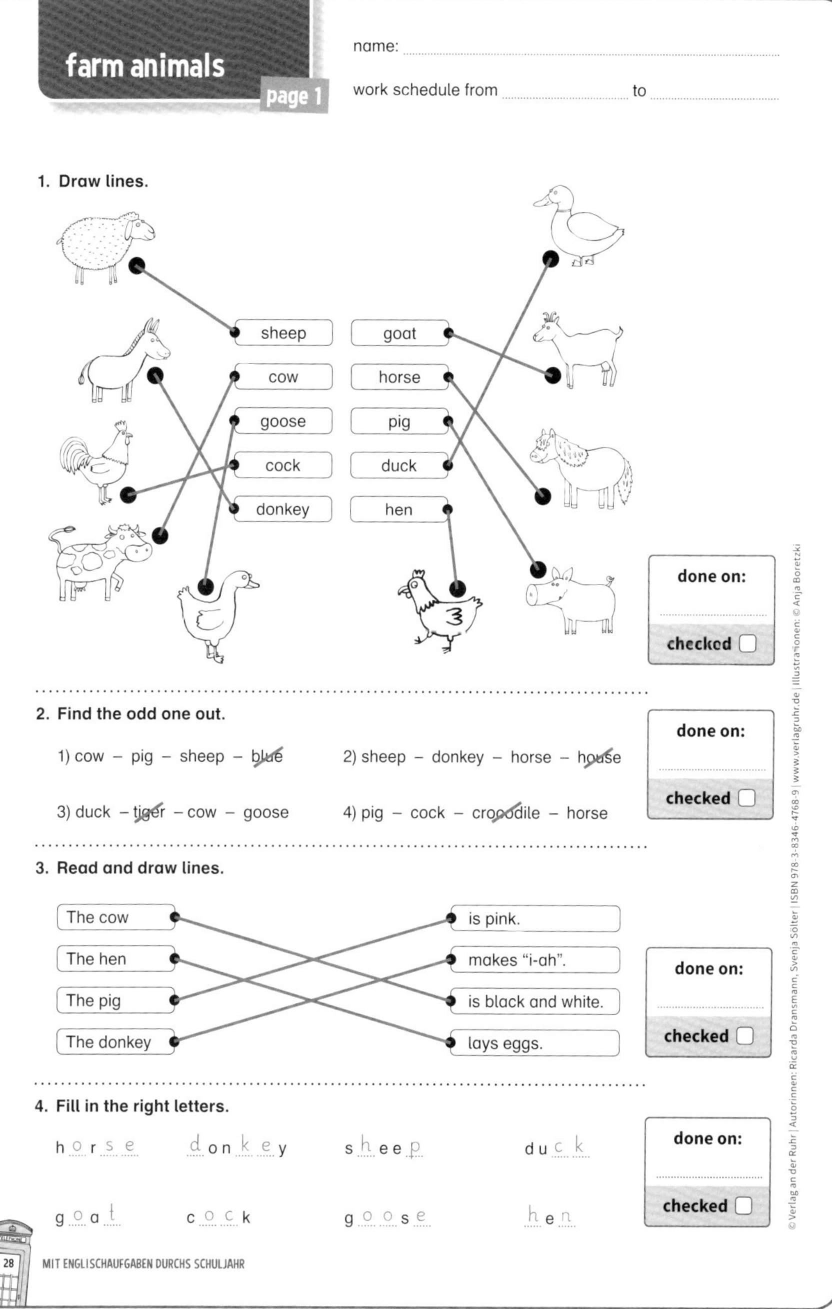

## farm animals
page 1

name: ..................

work schedule from .................. to ..................

**1. Draw lines.**

sheep — cow — goose — cock — donkey

goat — horse — pig — duck — hen

done on: checked

**2. Find the odd one out.**

1) cow – pig – sheep – ~~blue~~

2) sheep – donkey – horse – ~~house~~

3) duck – ~~tiger~~ – cow – goose

4) pig – cock – ~~crocodile~~ – horse

done on: checked

**3. Read and draw lines.**

The cow — is pink.

The hen — makes "i-ah".

The pig — is black and white.

The donkey — lays eggs.

done on: checked

**4. Fill in the right letters.**

horse — donkey — sheep — duck

goat — cock — goose — hen

done on: checked





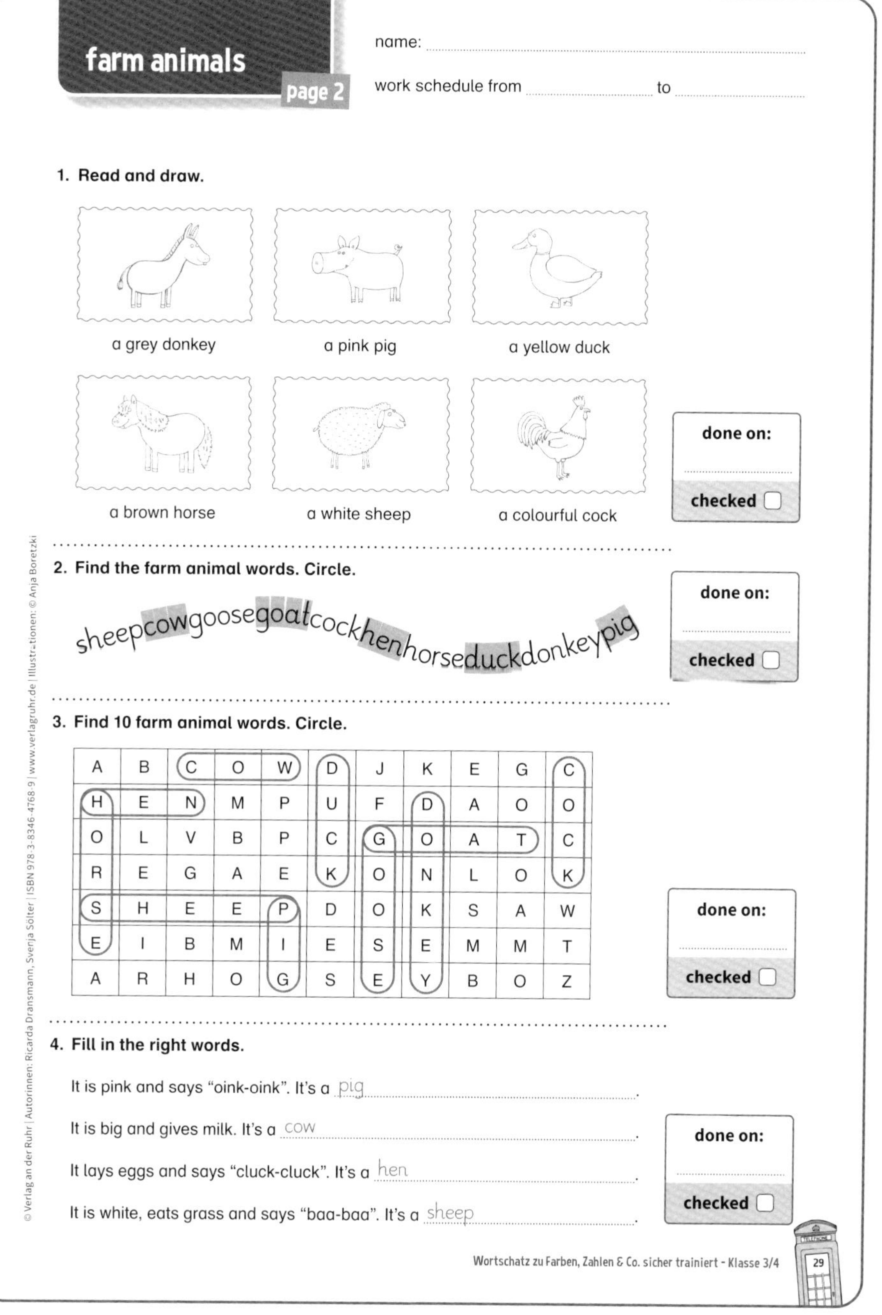

## farm animals
page 2

name: ..................

work schedule from .................. to ..................

**1. Read and draw.**

a grey donkey — a pink pig — a yellow duck

a brown horse — a white sheep — a colourful cock

done on: checked

**2. Find the farm animal words. Circle.**

sheepcowgoosegoatcockhenhorseduckdonkeypig

done on: checked

**3. Find 10 farm animal words. Circle.**

| A | B | C | O | W | D | J | K | E | G | C |
|---|---|---|---|---|---|---|---|---|---|---|
| H | E | N | M | P | U | F | D | A | O | O |
| O | L | V | B | P | C | G | O | A | T | C |
| R | E | G | A | E | K | O | N | L | O | K |
| S | H | E | E | P | D | O | K | S | A | W |
| E | I | B | M | I | E | S | E | M | M | T |
| A | R | H | O | G | S | E | Y | B | O | Z |

done on: checked

**4. Fill in the right words.**

It is pink and says "oink-oink". It's a pig.

It is big and gives milk. It's a cow.

It lays eggs and says "cluck-cluck". It's a hen.

It is white, eats grass and says "baa-baa". It's a sheep.

done on: checked

## hobbies & sports
**page 2**

name: ..........

work schedule from .......... to ..........

**1. Tick ✓ the right box.**

- [x] play football
- [ ] play tennis
- [ ] play the piano

- [x] play computer games
- [ ] play tennis
- [ ] play the guitar

- [x] go swimming
- [ ] read a book
- [ ] ride a bike

- [ ] dance
- [ ] ride a bike
- [x] ride a horse

done on: ..........
checked ☐

**2. What hobby is it? Look and write.**

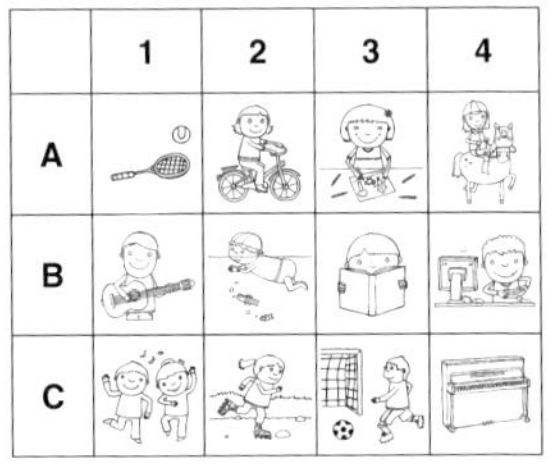

| | 1 | 2 | 3 | 4 |
|---|---|---|---|---|
| A | | | | |
| B | | | | |
| C | | | | |

A1 play tennis

A2 ride a bike

B1 play the guitar

B3 read a book

C1 dance

C4 play the piano

done on: ..........
checked ☐

**3. Tick ✓ your answer.** example

Can you …

| | | |
|---|---|---|
| … play tennis? | ☐ Yes, I can. | ☑ No, I can't. |
| … play the guitar? | ☑ Yes, I can. | ☐ No, I can't. |
| … ride a bike? | ☑ Yes, I can. | ☐ No, I can't. |
| … dance? | ☑ Yes, I can. | ☐ No, I can't. |

done on: ..........
checked ☐

**4. Right or wrong? Tick ✓ or ✗.**

- ✓ A boy is playing football.
- ✗ Two kids are swimming.
- ✓ A girl is playing tennis.
- ✓ Two kids are dancing.
- ✗ A boy is playing the guitar.
- ✗ Two kids are riding a bike.

done on: ..........
checked ☐

© Verlag an der Ruhr | Autorinnen: Ricarda Dransmann, Svenja Sölter | ISBN 978-3-8346-4768-9 | www.verlagruhr.de | Illustrationen: © Anja Boretzki, © Bettina Weyland (Wimmelbild)



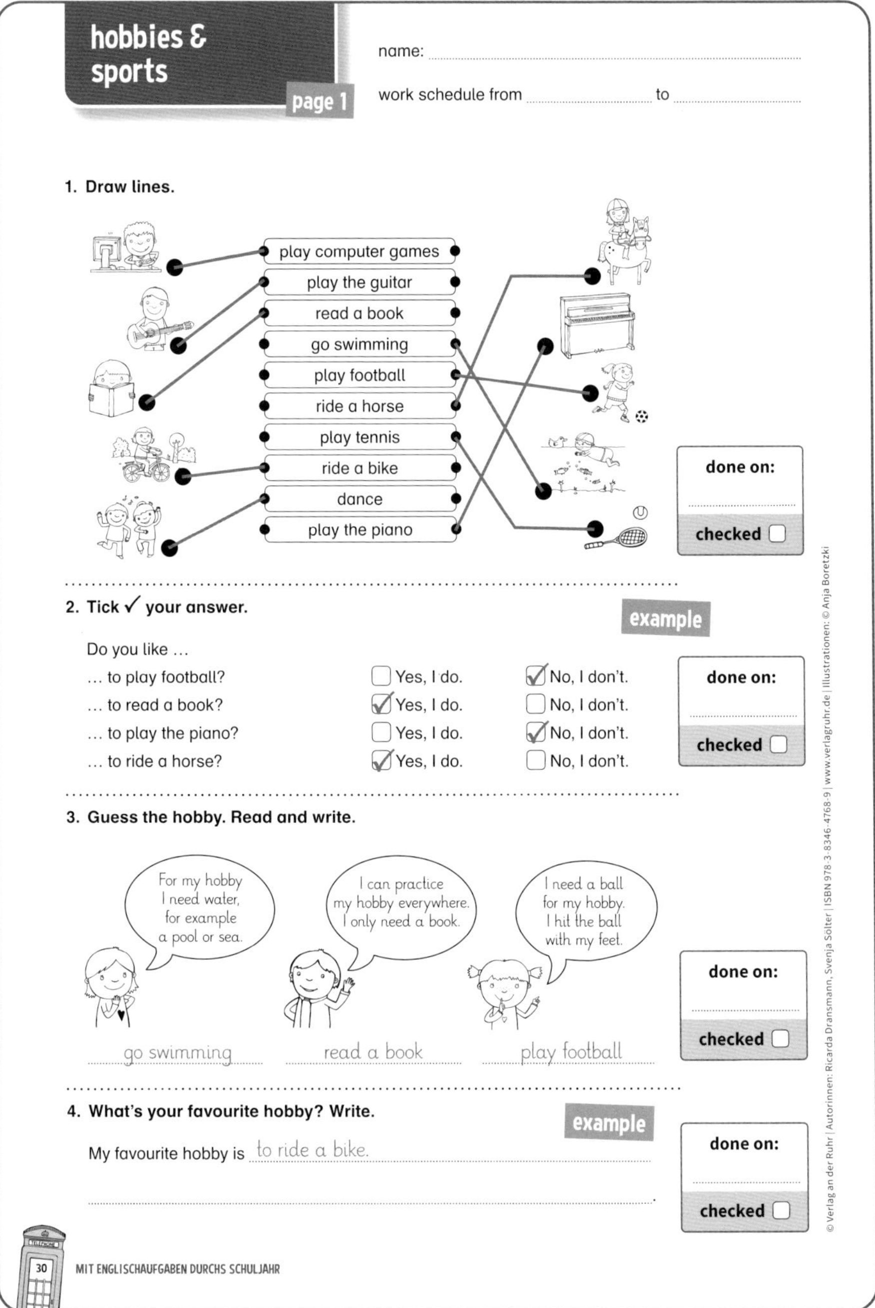

## hobbies & sports
**page 1**

name: ..........

work schedule from .......... to ..........

**1. Draw lines.**

- play computer games
- play the guitar
- read a book
- go swimming
- play football
- ride a horse
- play tennis
- ride a bike
- dance
- play the piano

done on: ..........
checked ☐

**2. Tick ✓ your answer.** example

Do you like …

| | | |
|---|---|---|
| … to play football? | ☐ Yes, I do. | ☑ No, I don't. |
| … to read a book? | ☑ Yes, I do. | ☐ No, I don't. |
| … to play the piano? | ☐ Yes, I do. | ☑ No, I don't. |
| … to ride a horse? | ☑ Yes, I do. | ☐ No, I don't. |

done on: ..........
checked ☐

**3. Guess the hobby. Read and write.**



go swimming — read a book — play football

done on: ..........
checked ☐

**4. What's your favourite hobby? Write.** example

My favourite hobby is to ride a bike.

done on: ..........
checked ☐

© Verlag an der Ruhr | Autorinnen: Ricarda Dransmann, Svenja Sölter | ISBN 978-3-8346-4768-9 | www.verlagruhr.de | Illustrationen: © Anja Boretzki

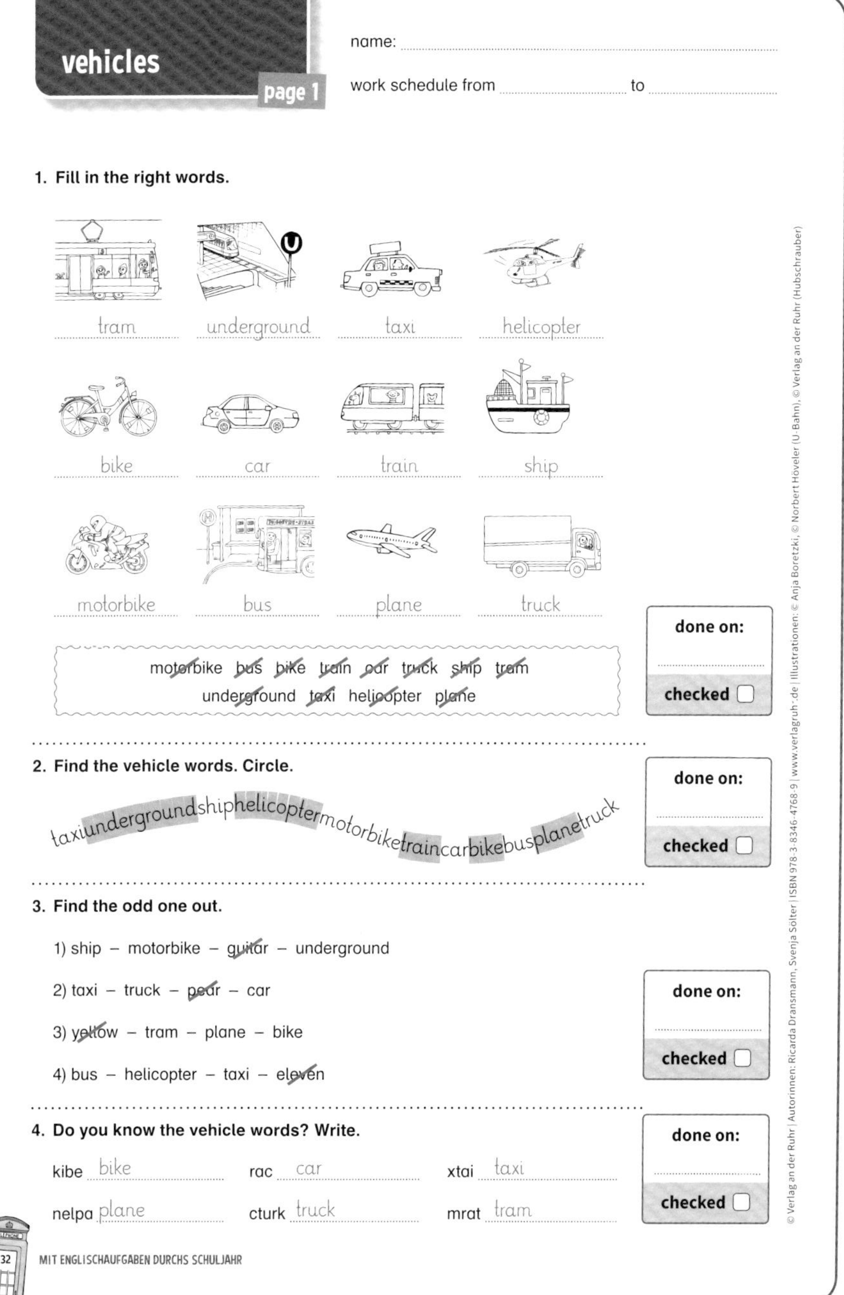

## vehicles
page 1

name: ..................

work schedule from .......... to ..........

1. Fill in the right words.

tram — underground — taxi — helicopter

bike — car — train — ship

motorbike — bus — plane — truck

motorbike ~~bus~~ ~~bike~~ ~~train~~ ~~car~~ ~~truck~~ ~~ship~~ ~~tram~~
underground ~~taxi~~ helicopter ~~plane~~

done on: ..........
checked ☐

2. Find the vehicle words. Circle.

taxiundergroundshiphelicoptermotorbiketraincarbikebusplanetruck

done on: ..........
checked ☐

3. Find the odd one out.

1) ship – motorbike – ~~guitar~~ – underground

2) taxi – truck – ~~pear~~ – car

3) ~~yellow~~ – tram – plane – bike

4) bus – helicopter – taxi – ~~eleven~~

done on: ..........
checked ☐

4. Do you know the vehicle words? Write.

kibe bike — rac car — xtai taxi

nelpa plane — cturk truck — mrat tram

done on: ..........
checked ☐

© Verlag an der Ruhr | Autorinnen: Ricarda Dransmann, Svenja Sölter | ISBN 978-3-8346-4768-9 | www.verlagruhr.de | Illustrationen: © Anja Boretzki, © Norbert Höveler (U-Bahn), © Verlag an der Ruhr (Hubschrauber)



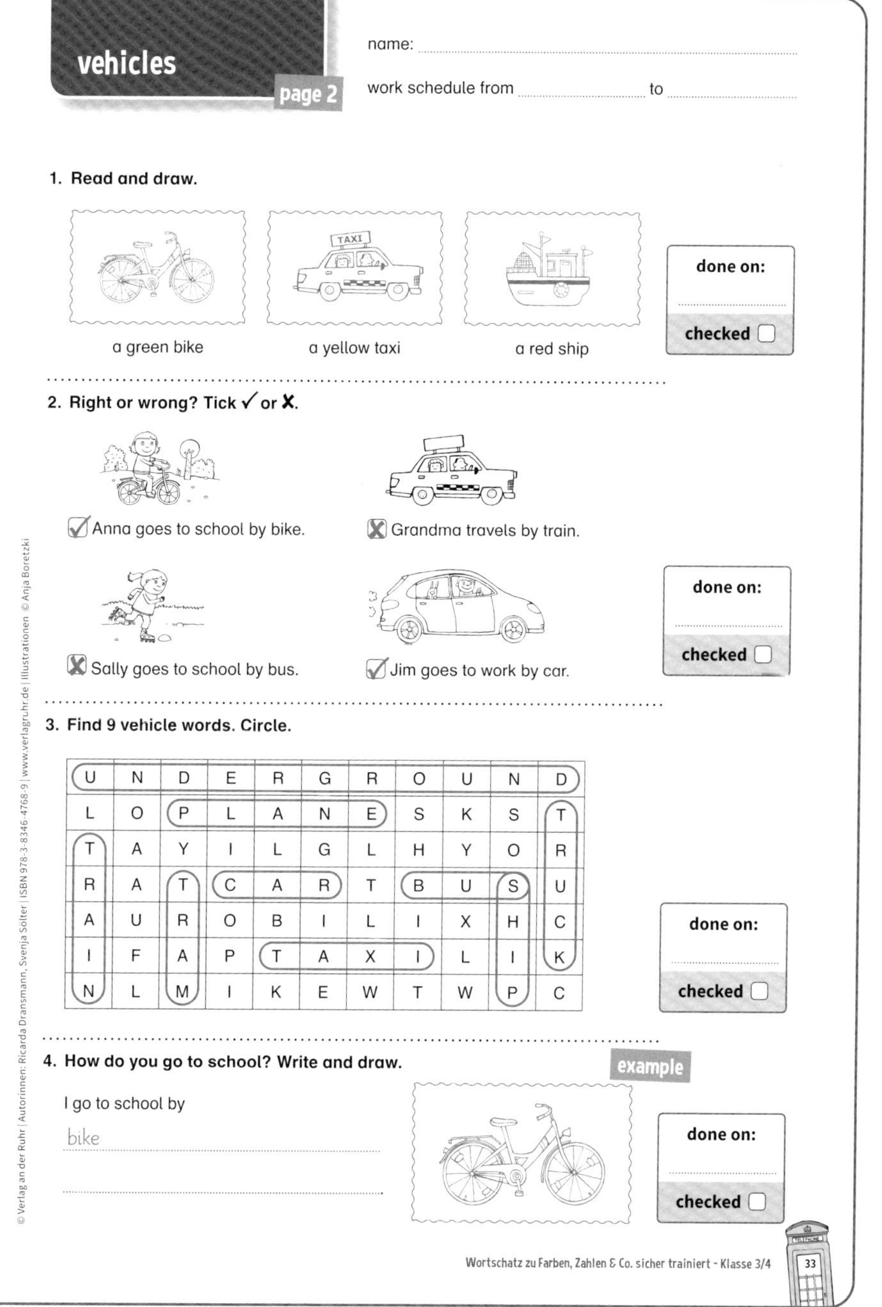

## vehicles
page 2

name: ..................

work schedule from .......... to ..........

1. Read and draw.

a green bike — a yellow taxi — a red ship

done on: ..........
checked ☐

2. Right or wrong? Tick ✓ or ✗.

☑ Anna goes to school by bike.

☒ Grandma travels by train.

☒ Sally goes to school by bus.

☑ Jim goes to work by car.

done on: ..........
checked ☐

3. Find 9 vehicle words. Circle.

| U | N | D | E | R | G | R | O | U | N | D |
|---|---|---|---|---|---|---|---|---|---|---|
| L | O | P | L | A | N | E | S | K | S | T |
| T | A | Y | I | L | G | L | H | Y | O | R |
| R | A | T | C | A | R | T | B | U | S | U |
| A | U | R | O | B | I | L | I | X | H | C |
| I | F | A | P | T | A | X | I | L | I | K |
| N | L | M | I | K | E | W | T | W | P | C |

done on: ..........
checked ☐

4. How do you go to school? Write and draw.

example

I go to school by

bike

done on: ..........
checked ☐

© Verlag an der Ruhr | Autorinnen: Ricarda Dransmann, Svenja Sölter | ISBN 978-3-8346-4768-9 | www.verlagruhr.de | Illustrationen: © Anja Boretzki



# Lösungen

# Lösungen

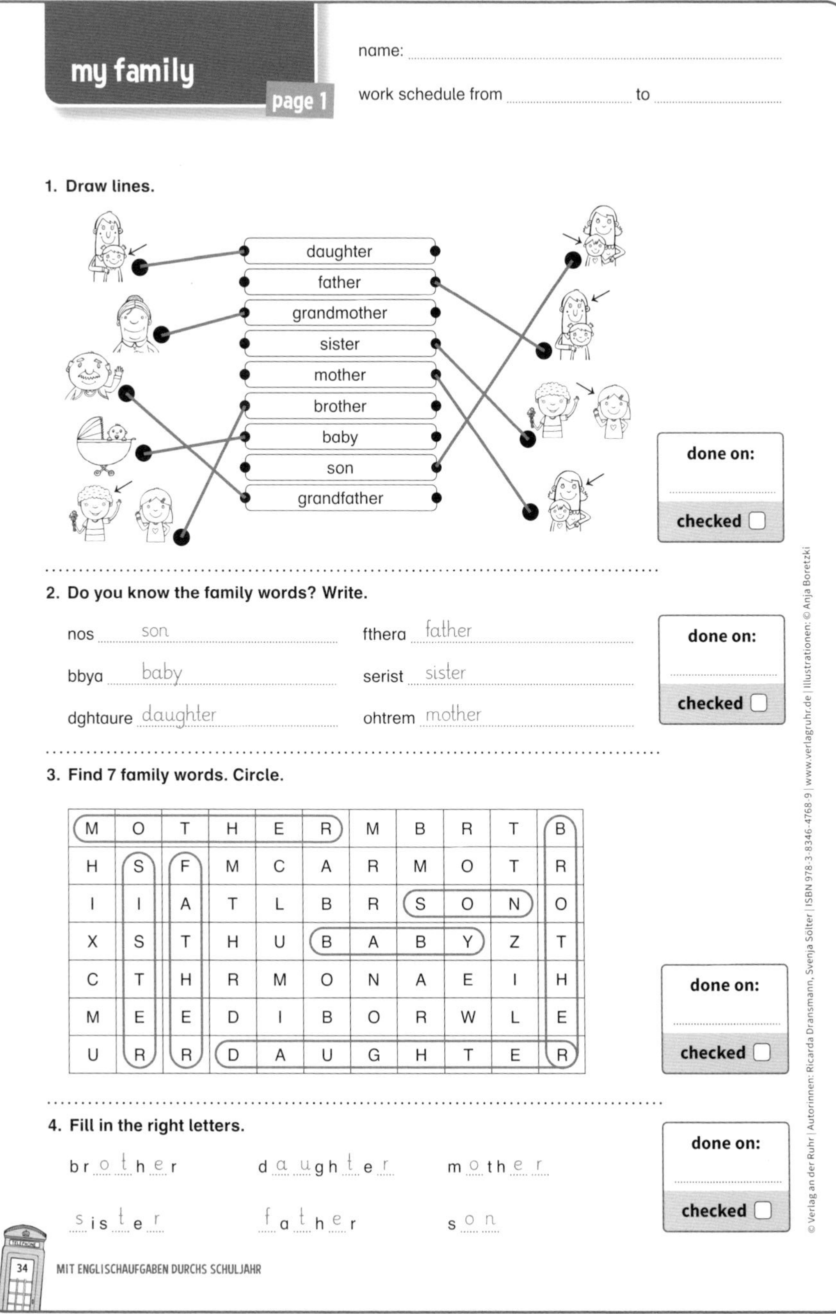

## my family page 1

name: ……

work schedule from …… to ……

1. Draw lines.



done on: …… checked ☐

2. Do you know the family words? Write.

nos son

bbya baby

dghtaure daughter

fthera father

serist sister

ohtrem mother

done on: …… checked ☐

3. Find 7 family words. Circle.

| | | | | | | | | | | |
|---|---|---|---|---|---|---|---|---|---|---|
| M | O | T | H | E | R | M | B | R | T | B |
| H | S | F | M | C | A | R | M | O | T | R |
| I | I | A | T | L | B | R | S | O | N | O |
| X | S | T | H | U | B | A | B | Y | Z | T |
| C | T | H | R | M | O | N | A | E | I | H |
| M | E | E | D | I | B | O | R | W | L | E |
| U | R | R | D | A | U | G | H | T | E | R |

done on: …… checked ☐

4. Fill in the right letters.

brother    daughter    mother

sister    father    son

done on: …… checked ☐



© Verlag an der Ruhr | Autorinnen: Ricarda Dransmann, Svenja Sölter | ISBN 978-3-8346-4768-9 | www.verlagruhr.de | Illustrationen: © Anja Boretzki

## my family page 2

name: ……

work schedule from …… to ……

1. Draw lines.

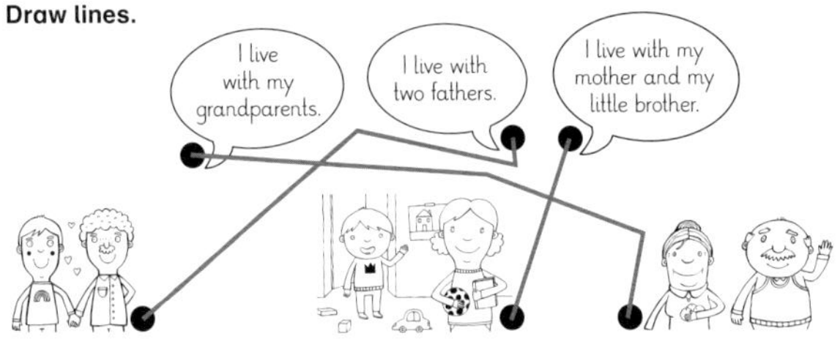

done on: …… checked ☐

2. Find the family words. Circle.

fatherbrotherbabysistermothergrandmotherdaughtersongrandfather

done on: …… checked ☐

3. This is Mia's family tree. Who is it? Write.

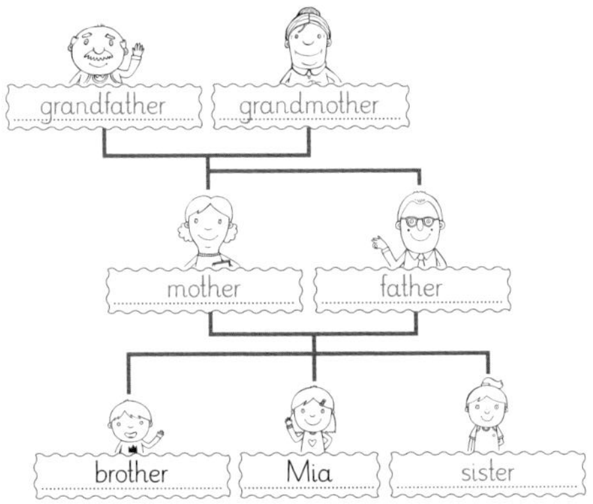

done on: …… checked ☐

4. Who do you live with? Draw and write.

example

I live with my mother, my father, my brother and my sister.

done on: …… checked ☐

© Verlag an der Ruhr | Autorinnen: Ricarda Dransmann, Svenja Sölter | ISBN 978-3-8346-4768-9 | www.verlagruhr.de | Illustrationen: © Anja Boretzki

# Lösungen

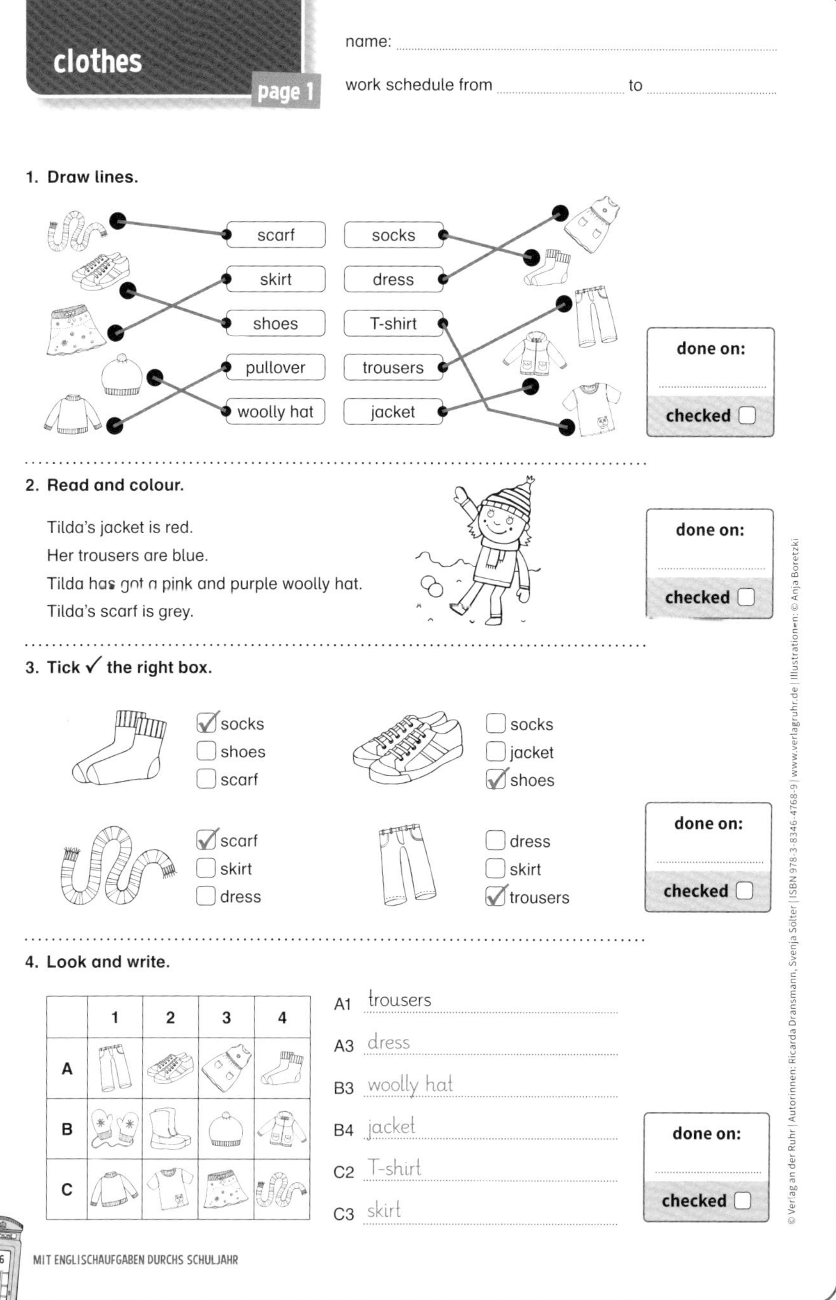

## clothes

page 1

name: ..........

work schedule from .......... to ..........

**1. Draw lines.**

scarf, skirt, shoes, pullover, woolly hat

socks, dress, T-shirt, trousers, jacket

done on: checked ☐

**2. Read and colour.**

Tilda's jacket is red.
Her trousers are blue.
Tilda has got a pink and purple woolly hat.
Tilda's scarf is grey.

done on: checked ☐

**3. Tick ✓ the right box.**

✓ socks ☐ shoes ☐ scarf

✓ scarf ☐ skirt ☐ dress

☐ socks ☐ jacket ✓ shoes

☐ dress ☐ skirt ✓ trousers

done on: checked ☐

**4. Look and write.**

| | 1 | 2 | 3 | 4 |
|---|---|---|---|---|
| A | | | | |
| B | | | | |
| C | | | | |

A1 trousers
A3 dress
B3 woolly hat
B4 jacket
C2 T-shirt
C3 skirt

done on: checked ☐

MIT ENGLISCHAUFGABEN DURCHS SCHULJAHR

36



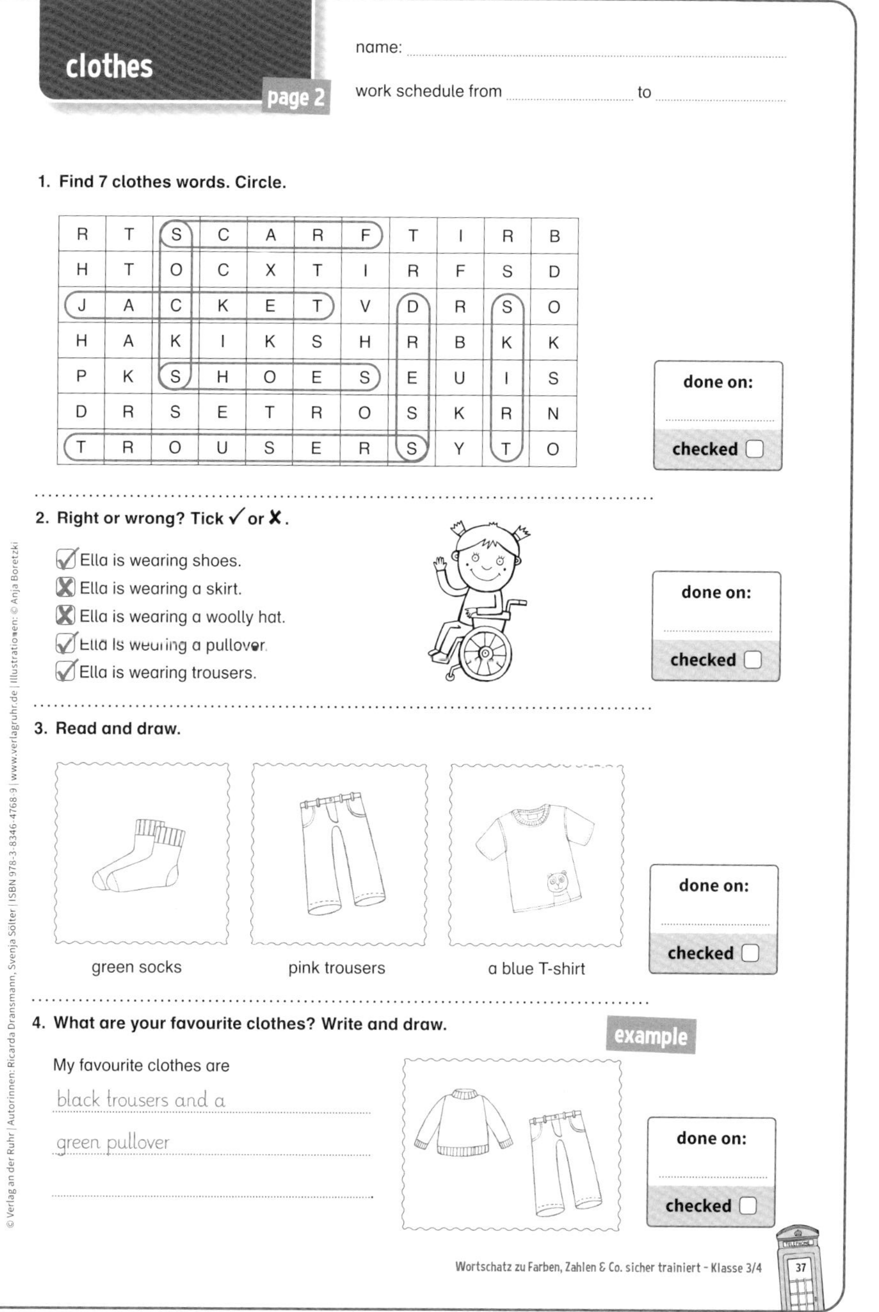

## clothes

page 2

name: ..........

work schedule from .......... to ..........

**1. Find 7 clothes words. Circle.**

| | | | | | | | | | | |
|---|---|---|---|---|---|---|---|---|---|---|
| R | T | S | C | A | R | F | T | I | R | B |
| H | T | O | C | X | T | I | R | F | S | D |
| J | A | C | K | E | T | V | D | R | S | O |
| H | A | K | I | K | S | H | R | B | K | K |
| P | K | S | H | O | E | S | E | U | I | S |
| D | R | S | E | T | R | O | S | K | R | N |
| T | R | O | U | S | E | R | S | Y | T | O |

done on: checked ☐

**2. Right or wrong? Tick ✓ or ✗.**

✓ Ella is wearing shoes.
✗ Ella is wearing a skirt.
✗ Ella is wearing a woolly hat.
✓ Ella is wearing a pullover.
✓ Ella is wearing trousers.

done on: checked ☐

**3. Read and draw.**

green socks — pink trousers — a blue T-shirt

done on: checked ☐

**4. What are your favourite clothes? Write and draw.**

example

My favourite clothes are
black trousers and a
green pullover

done on: checked ☐

Wortschatz zu Farben, Zahlen & Co. sicher trainiert - Klasse 3/4

37

# Lösungen

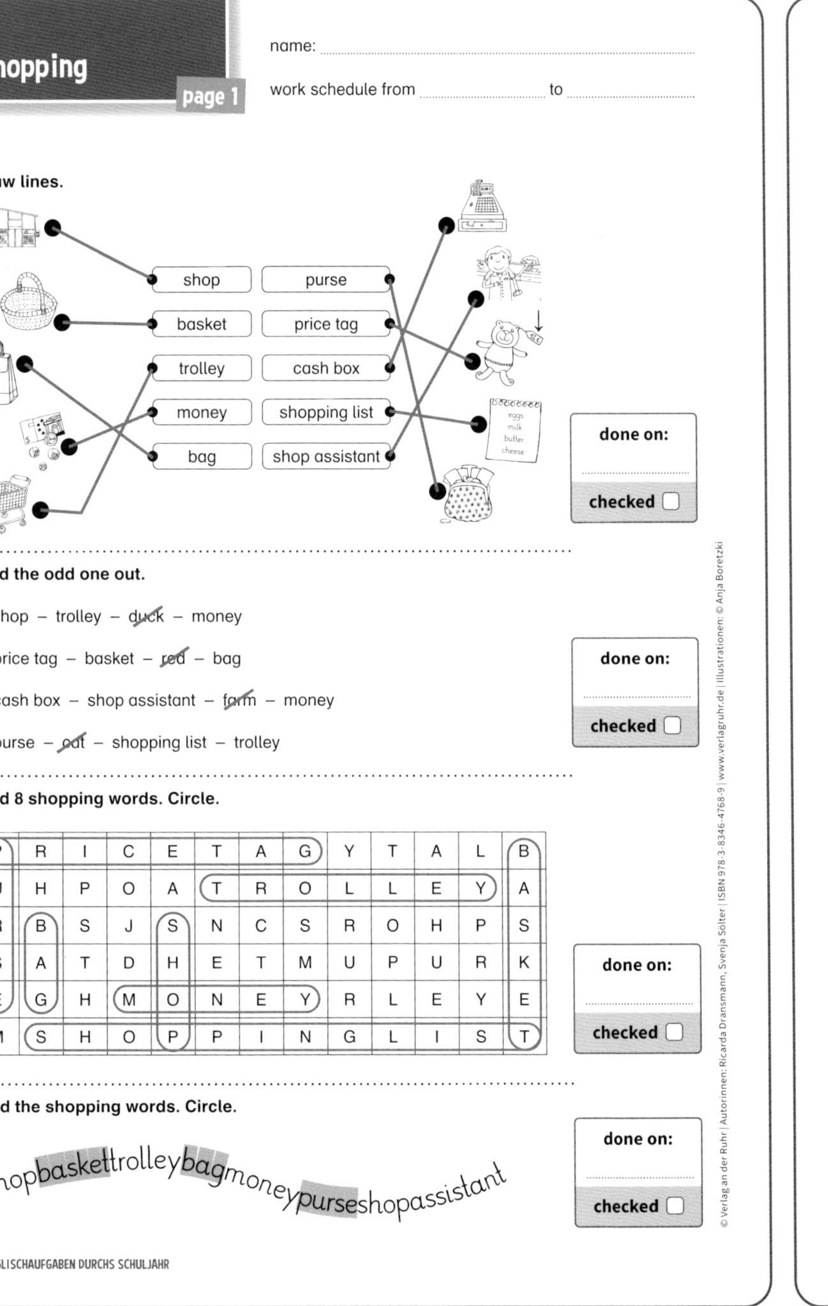

**shopping** page 1

name: ..........

work schedule from .......... to ..........

1. **Draw lines.**

shop — basket — trolley — money — bag

purse — price tag — cash box — shopping list — shop assistant



done on: .......... checked ☐

2. **Find the odd one out.**

1) shop – trolley – ~~duck~~ – money

2) price tag – basket – ~~red~~ – bag

3) cash box – shop assistant – ~~farm~~ – money

4) purse – ~~cat~~ – shopping list – trolley

done on: .......... checked ☐

3. **Find 8 shopping words. Circle.**

| | | | | | | | | | | | | |
|---|---|---|---|---|---|---|---|---|---|---|---|---|
| P | R | I | C | E | T | A | G | Y | T | A | L | B |
| U | H | P | O | A | T | R | O | L | L | E | Y | A |
| R | B | S | J | S | N | C | S | R | O | H | P | S |
| S | A | T | D | H | E | T | M | U | P | U | R | K |
| E | G | H | M | O | N | E | Y | R | L | E | Y | E |
| M | S | H | O | P | P | I | N | G | L | I | S | T |

done on: .......... checked ☐

4. **Find the shopping words. Circle.**

shopbaskettrolleybagmoneypurseshopassistant

done on: .......... checked ☐

© Verlag an der Ruhr | Autorinnen: Ricarda Dransmann, Svenja Solter | ISBN 978-3-8346-4768-9 | www.verlagruhr.de | Illustrationen: © Anja Boretzki



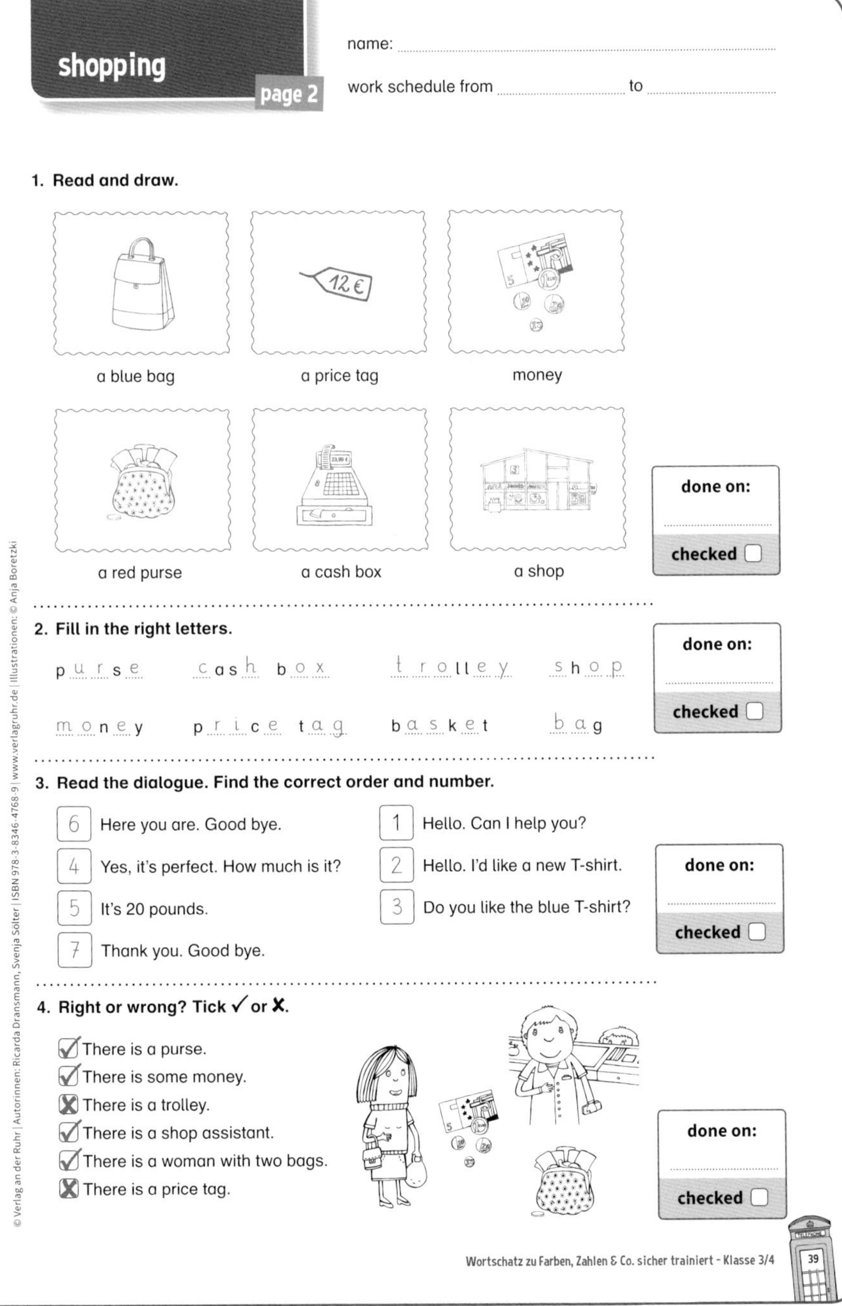

**shopping** page 2

name: ..........

work schedule from .......... to ..........

1. **Read and draw.**

a blue bag — a price tag — money

a red purse — a cash box — a shop

done on: .......... checked ☐

2. **Fill in the right letters.**

purse — cash box — trolley — shop

money — price tag — basket — bag

done on: .......... checked ☐

3. **Read the dialogue. Find the correct order and number.**

6 Here you are. Good bye.

4 Yes, it's perfect. How much is it?

5 It's 20 pounds.

7 Thank you. Good bye.

1 Hello. Can I help you?

2 Hello. I'd like a new T-shirt.

3 Do you like the blue T-shirt?

done on: .......... checked ☐

4. **Right or wrong? Tick ✓ or ✗.**

✓ There is a purse.

✓ There is some money.

✗ There is a trolley.

✓ There is a shop assistant.

✓ There is a woman with two bags.

✗ There is a price tag.

done on: .......... checked ☐

© Verlag an der Ruhr | Autorinnen: Ricarda Dransmann, Svenja Solter | ISBN 978-3-8346-4768-9 | www.verlagruhr.de | Illustrationen: © Anja Boretzki

# Lösungen

## the time — page 1

name: ..........

work schedule from .......... to ..........

**1. Draw lines.**

- It's half past one.
- It's eleven o'clock.
- It's a quarter to ten.
- It's half past nine.
- It's a quarter past twelve.
- It's seven o'clock.

done on: ..........
checked ☐

**2. Read and draw.**

It's two o'clock. It's five o'clock. It's twelve o'clock.

It's half past three. It's a quarter past six. It's a quarter to seven.

done on: ..........
checked ☐

**3. What time is it? Look and write.**

| | 1 | 2 | 3 | 4 |
|---|---|---|---|---|
| A | | | | |
| B | | | | |
| C | | | | |

A1 It's a quarter past twelve.
A3 It's half past two.
B1 It's four o'clock.
B4 It's half past six.
C1 It's a quarter past eight.
C4 It's a quarter to twelve.

done on: ..........
checked ☐

**4. Answer the questions.** example

When do you get up? I get up at seven o'clock.
When do you go to school? I go to school at eight o'clock.
When do you have lunch? I have lunch at half past twelve.
When do you go to bed? I go to bed at nine o'clock.

done on: ..........
checked ☐



© Verlag an der Ruhr | Autorinnen: Ricarda Dransmann, Svenja Sölter | ISBN 978-3-8346-4768-9 | www.verlagruhr.de | Illustrationen: © Max Diesel – stock.adobe.com, © Anja Boretzki (Telefonzelle)

## the time — page 2

name: ..........

work schedule from .......... to ..........

**1. Tick ✓ the right answer.**

☐ It's four o'clock.
☑ It's five o'clock.
☐ It's three o'clock.

☐ It's half past six.
☐ It's half past eight.
☑ It's half past seven.

☐ It's a quarter to three.
☑ It's a quarter past three.
☐ It's a quarter past four.

☐ It's a quarter to eight.
☐ It's a quarter past nine.
☑ It's a quarter to nine.

done on: ..........
checked ☐

**2. What time is it? Write.**

6:00 — It's six o'clock.
9:30 — It's half past nine.
8:15 — It's a quarter past eight.
2:45 — It's a quarter to three.

done on: ..........
checked ☐

**3. Read. Tick ✓ the right box.**

I go to school at eight o'clock. ☐ 9:00 ☑ 8:00 ☐ 8:30
I get up at a quarter to seven. ☑ 6:45 ☐ 6:30 ☐ 7:00
I have lunch at half past twelve. ☐ 11:30 ☑ 12:30 ☐ 12:00

done on: ..........
checked ☐

**4. What time is it? Read and write.**

two o'clock + two hours = four o'clock
six o'clock + 15 minutes = a quarter past six
seven o'clock + 30 minutes = half past seven
ten o'clock + 1 hour and 45 minutes = a quarter to twelve

done on: ..........
checked ☐

© Verlag an der Ruhr | Autorinnen: Ricarda Dransmann, Svenja Sölter | ISBN 978-3-8346-4768-9 | www.verlagruhr.de | Illustrationen: © Max Diesel – stock.adobe.com, © Anja Boretzki (Telefonzelle)

# Lösungen

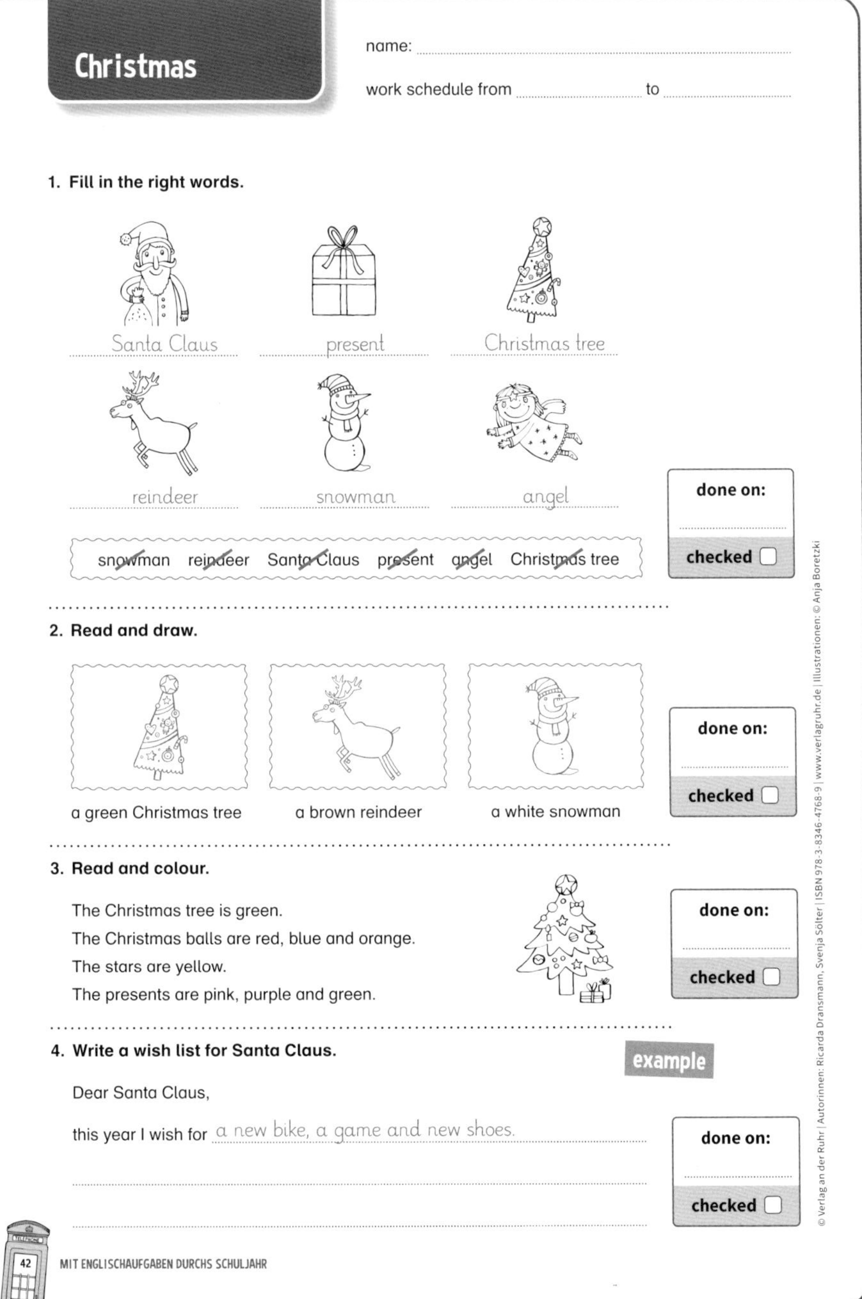

## Christmas

name: ..............................

work schedule from .................... to ....................

**1. Fill in the right words.**

Santa Claus — present — Christmas tree

reindeer — snowman — angel

snowman reindeer Santa Claus present angel Christmas tree

done on: ....... checked ☐

**2. Read and draw.**

a green Christmas tree — a brown reindeer — a white snowman

done on: ....... checked ☐

**3. Read and colour.**

The Christmas tree is green.
The Christmas balls are red, blue and orange.
The stars are yellow.
The presents are pink, purple and green.

done on: ....... checked ☐

**4. Write a wish list for Santa Claus.** example

Dear Santa Claus,

this year I wish for a new bike, a game and new shoes.

done on: ....... checked ☐





## Easter

name: ..............................

work schedule from .................... to ....................

**1. Fill in the right words.**

chick — grass — Easter egg

Easter bunny — hen — nest

hen grass Easter egg nest Easter bunny chick

done on: ....... checked ☐

**2. Find the Easter words. Circle.**

Easterbunnygrassnesthen Eastereggchick

done on: ....... checked ☐

**3. Find 6 Easter words. Circle.**

| E | A | S | T | E | R | B | U | N | N | Y |
|---|---|---|---|---|---|---|---|---|---|---|
| A | C | H | I | C | K | I | F | G | F | E |
| T | L | E | A | S | L | A | T | D | N | A |
| S | J | N | Y | G | E | A | H | S | E | T |
| B | W | E | B | R | J | B | L | T | S | R |
| F | A | S | N | A | Y | M | K | E | T | S |
| E | Y | E | A | S | T | E | R | E | G | G |
| G | E | R | A | S | D | C | I | C | K | D |

done on: ....... checked ☐

**4. Read and draw.**

There is green grass.
There is the Easter bunny.
I can see three nests with lots of Easter eggs.
Two Easter eggs are red.
Three Easter eggs are blue.

done on: ....... checked ☐